HOW TO BUILD BUSINESS CREDIT AND GET ACCESS TO FUNDING

Copyright

Credit Report
Credit score range:
Your Credit Score:
Excellent
760
Late payments:

Table of Contents

OVERVIEW

This Business Credit & Funding Guide was assembled by a team of business owners and entrepreneurs who understand the power of leveraging business credit. Many of the contributors to this guide gained this knowledge the hard way through trial and error and a host of mistakes, denials, and missed opportunities along the way.

The great news is by following this guide, you'll get an opportunity to bypass majority of the "red tape" and be in position to realize success much sooner than most! The wealthy have understood and exercised the information and concepts in this guide for generations, and now you can too!

One of your main goals should be to obtain assets through your business without these assets being attached to you personally, so you can minimize the risks and liabilities these assets may carry. How is this done? We're glad you asked...the process is simple. Not easy, but simple!

The first step is (DO NOT SKIP THIS STEP) to have a solid personal credit profile. As you are starting out in business, most likely, lenders and creditors will pull your personal credit to validate and justify any extension of debt they offer you. In many cases, you will have to personally guarantee (PG) the debt.

The second step is to follow this guide to the "T." Throughout the process, you will learn that accounts established using your business EIN, even if they are personally guaranteed, typically do not report on your personal credit profile. This simple piece of information, if exercised properly, should allow you to rinse and repeat the cycle of obtaining business funding and assets. Eventually, as your business grows and establishes credibility, it will no longer need a personal guarantor, which disconnects your personal ties and provides you an extra layer of protection.

As you go through this guide, please remember it is not whether you know the information, or you've heard it before, you must apply it. We wish you the best and hope this guide assists you in reaching your fullest potential!

Set Up Your Business the Right Way

Chapter 1. What is Business Credit?

Business Credit is credit obtained in a Business Name. With business credit, the Business builds its own credit profile and credit score. With an established credit profile and score, the business will then qualify for credit. This credit is based on the business's ability to pay, and not the business owners. Since the business qualifies for the credit, in some cases there is no personal guarantee required from the business owner.

You must actively work to build business credit. But you can do it easily and quickly – much faster than building consumer credit scores. vendor credit is a big part of this process. If you try to do the steps out of order, you will be turned down repeatedly.

Fortunately, we know the steps to take. And we know the order in which you need to take them.

There are a ton of benefits that business credit provides. This includes that you can build a credit profile for a business that is completely separate from your personal credit profile. This effectively gives you DOUBLE the borrowing power as they have both personal and business credit profiles built.

Business credit scores are based only on whether the business pays its bills on time. You can get credit much faster using their business credit profile versus their personal credit profile. Approval limits are much higher on business accounts versus personal accounts. This is yet another benefit. Per SBA, credit limits on business cards are usually 10 – 100 times higher than consumer credit.

The business can use its credit to qualify for credit cards from major retailers, even MasterCard or Visa. The business can also qualify for credit lines and loans.

When done right, you can build business credit without a personal guarantee. You can get business credit quickly, regardless of personal credit quality. Plus, you can get a lot of business credit without taking on personal liability, or a personal guarantee. This means in case of default; your personal assets can't be pursued.

Chapter 2. Business Credibility

One of the most important parts to establishing your business credibility is making sure ALL your business records list the same business information.

Anyone can pull your business credit. It is unlike personal credit where a signed authorization needs to take place. When someone pulls your business credit, they can view many intimate details about your business.

Lenders verify these details during the underwriting process. Mismatched records are one of the most common reasons a fundable deal is declined.

This guide will assist you in setting up your business the

right way!

Let's get started!

Chapter 3. Business Entity

To establish business credibility, you first must have a business! One of the first steps is to officially file/register your entity with the Secretary of State in your headquarter state. If you are filing in a state other than your headquarter state, be sure to foreign file in your headquarter state too. Lenders will need to see a paper trail to your local state.

The filing process and fees are different in every state. Some states require your entity to be renewed annually to stay in good standing. Keep your entity updated with your correct business information including your address and ownership. Your business entity is the beginning process of establishing credibility so do it right. Make sure to consider all the following items before you file because some will need to be included in your filing:

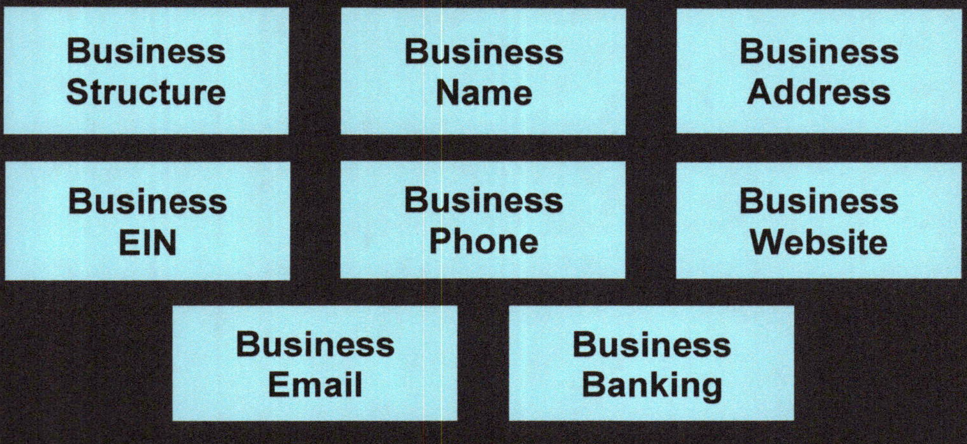

Chapter 4. Business Structure

When setting up your business entity you will likely ask yourself what type of entity you should establish. Each entity has their own tax and liability differences.

There are four (4) major structure types:
Corporation - generally for more larger, complex, and established companies with employees

Limited Liability Company (LLC) - offers efficient tax options, limited liability, and the flexibility of partnerships

Sole proprietorship - owner is personally liable and responsible for the business. Many people don't consider a sole proprietorship or DBA as an actual business entity.

Partnership - several variations will allow parties to combine into a partnership

Weigh the options and understand the tax and legal benefits to each option. There are many useful resources to help you.

Sba.gov does agree at job explaining each structure in detail.
Visit: https://www.sba.gov/business-guide/launch-your- business/choose-business-structure

Chapter 5. Business Name

Selecting the right business name for you and your product/service is super important because it is one of the first ways others identify with you and your brand.

Before you purchase your domain, build a website, or print business cards, make sure the name you select is available with your Secretary of State. You also may want to use sites such as namechk.com to check the name availability across social platforms.

Consider a few business names in case your first choice is unavailable.

Once you make your business name selection, make sure you are consistent with the exact spelling, punctuation, etc. across all business filings and accounts. This includes the Secretary of State, IRS, banking institutions, and other entities.
Name variations across accounts may raise concerns.

Lastly, be aware that there are some high-risk industries that may guarantee a decline with creditors. Additionally, using high-risk industry descriptions in your business name may limit your financing options. Consider adding words such as "Consultant" or "Enterprises" to the end of your business name to keep it somewhat general and keep financial institutions from placing your business on the restricted lists, which can impact your business.

Restricted industries (automatic decline) include:

• Ammunition or weapons manufacturing (wholesale and retail)
• Bail bonds
• Check cashing agencies
• Energy, oil trading, or petroleum extraction or production
• Finance: (federal reserve banks, foreign banks, banks, bank holding companies, loan brokers, commodity brokers, security brokers, mortgage brokers, mortgage bankers, mortgage companies, bail bond companies, or mutual fund managers)
• Gaming or gambling activities
• Loans for the speculative purchases of securities or goods
• Pawn shops
• Political campaigns, candidates, or committees
• Public administration (e.g.,city, county, state,and federal governmental agencies)
• X-rated products or entertainment

Be aware of these Restricted and High- Risk Industries

High-Risk Industries (subject to stricter underwriting guidelines):

- Agriculture or forest products
- Auto, recreational vehicle or boat sales
- Courier services
- Computer and software related services
- Dry cleaners
- Entertainment (adult entertainment is to be considered restricted)
- General contractors
- Gasoline stations or convenience stores (also known as c-stores)
- Healthcare; specifically nursing homes, assisted living facilities, and continuing care retirement centers
- Special trade contractors
- Hotels or motels
- Jewelry, precious stones and metals; wholesale and retail
- Limousine services
- Long distance or "over-the-road" trucking
- Mobile or manufactured home sales
- Phone sales and direct selling establishments
- Real estate agents/brokers
- Real estate developers or land subdividers
- Restaurants or drinking establishments
- Software or programming companies
- Taxi cabs (including the purchase of cab medallions)
- Travel agencies

Chapter 6. Business Address

One aspect of the vetting process for most lenders is to verify your business address to see if in fact your business is a "real" business. As you can imagine, the more professional and legitimate your business is or appears to be, the better! Many lenders prefer that a business has an actual physical business location. Some lenders, specifically revenue-based lenders, may decline you if your business doesn't have a physical business location. Note: the business address you use should be one that you intend to use long-term.

Many lenders use USPS tools to verify business locations. Refrain from using an address that other businesses are using such as a P.O. Box or UPS address as your physical address. Lenders show concern when a P.O. Box or UPS address is listed as the only business address on file. You can use a P.O. Box or UPS address as an additional mailing address, but any documents and filings also should have a deliverable physical address.

- **Must be a real brick-and-mortar building**
- **Deliverable physical address**
- **Should not be a home address**
- **Should not be a P.O. Box**
- **Should not be a UPS address**

Your residential address can suffice as your business address in some cases, but it is not recommended, especially if you are looking to build and scale your business and maximize funding opportunities.

One budget friendly solution is securing a virtual office. Virtual offices can give your business a professional presence with a physical address, business phone number, meeting spaces, and other amenities without the high overhead costs of owning/renting a brick-and-mortar office.

Once you have established your business entity, the next step is to apply for your Employer Identification Number (EIN). Similar to your personal social security number, your business EIN is a nine-digit federal government identification number that you will use to identify your business for all future uses.

It is important to use the exact same business information when registering for your EIN that you used to establish your business entity. Lenders and other groups can verify against the information, and the slightest variance can result in declines or incorrect reporting.

APPLY FOR YOUR EIN

WWW.IRS.GOV

Chapter 8. Business Phone & 411 Listing

Lenders can see if your business phone number is a cell phone, residential number, or an actual business phone number. It boosts your business credibility to have an actual business phone number. Also, depending on your business model, it may be appropriate for you to have a 1- 800 number as well as a local business number.

There are many inexpensive virtual business phone services available.

After establishing your business phone number, we recommend you list it under the National
411 Directory, so lenders can verify your business more easily. Keep in mind that unfortunately, cell phone numbers can't be listed in the National 411 Directory.

You can go to listyourself.net or other similar services to list your business phone number. Once submitted, it takes about one week for your business phone number to be listed. Check to see if your phone number has been listed by dialing your area code and 555-1212. If you call from your cell phone, your cell phone company will forward you to their independent
411 service, so you should call the number from your business phone to verify.

Chapter 9. Business Website& Email

Lenders and potential customers likely will search for your website. A valid and operational website can boost your credibility drastically.

A business email address is equally important. An email address with your company domain appears more professional and credible than using a free or personal email address.

There are many options when building a website from professional services to do it yourself services.

Chapter 10. Business Licenses

Does your business need a license?
Every city, state, country may have different license requirements and filling processes. When you file your business entity, the state will tell you if a state license is required.
Go on your city website or call your city offices to see if your type of business requires a city business license.

If your type of business requires a license, file immediately to prevent delays.
Make sure you use your correct business information to set up your license. The business information on your license should match the information on all other business records to boost your credibility with lenders and others.

Renew your business license as required to stay in good standing.

Resources:

http://cityapplications.com/

Business Banking Accounts

Some people will say your business is not truly official until you have a business banking account. When you are establishing your business bank account, make sure your business information is correct and accurate including correct spelling and punctuation. It should be the same business info you have used on all other filings.

Note: Have you ever noticed how bankers seem to ask 101 questions when you go to open a new bank account? Yes, most bankers are friendly and want to establish a relationship with you, but they also are vetting you during this time, and they are trying to determine what categories and lists to place you on! Don't feel obligated to answer every question in extreme detail. It is okay to generalize some answers. (i.e."I am a consultant.") Don't get put on the restricted list!

Depending on your business, product/service, anticipated revenue, etc., it may be wise for you to establish a merchant account with your banking institution or another third party. Merchant accounts simply provide you the ability to accept credit and debit cards.

Having flexible payment options is a huge benefit to your business and the customer, and you'll notice customers tend to spend more with credit and debit card payment options.
Having a business merchant account also may increase financing opportunities down the road.

Chapter 1. Establishing Business Credit

Trade Accounts

Now that your business is set up and ready to roll, the next step is to start building business credit by establishing business trade accounts.

It is important to note that not all business creditors, lenders, vendors, etc. report your business credit history!

Trade accounts (sometimes referred to as vendor accounts) are typically store accounts in which a vendor extends credit to a business to purchase products/services, and the business pays for the goods later, which typically is negotiated with 30, 60, or 90 day net terms.

Once they are established, these trade accounts will begin reporting to the business credit reporting agencies and begin building your business credit profile. Lenders rely heavily on your business credit profile to help determine whether they are going to approve your loan amount and its terms. In fact, most of the lending decisions for small businesses are automated, and lenders use computers and complex algorithms in the underwriting process to verify your information and identify data points.

We recommend you establish and build these trade accounts in stages. At the end of this guide, we provide a detailed breakdown of various trade accounts that you may want to consider establishing, the data points lenders will be evaluating, and the stage at which we recommend establishing these accounts to build your business credit.

We also offer a Done for You Business Credit and Funding service at:

Premier1BusinessCredit.com

Chapter 2. Business Credit Reporting Agencies

Business Credit Reports

When you're trying to get a business loan, establish payment terms with a new vendor, or get any type of business credit, your business credit report can be a major factor in your success. This is why you should monitor it regularly!

Studies show that 72% of business owners don't know their business credit scores. If you're one of those business owners who don't know their scores, here are four great reasons to check your business credit on a regular basis:

Mistakes happen. Your business credit may get mixed up with the credit from another business, or one of your vendors or lenders may report incorrect information. If you don't check your report, you won't know.

Credit scores change. Every time new information is reported by your lenders and vendors, your credit reports and scores may change.

Fraud can occur. Business credit fraud or identity theft is a growing problem and may result in negative information on your reports. Monitoring your credit can alert you to suspicious activity.

 Business owners who understand their business credit profile are more likely to maximize their financing potential.

Currently, there are no companies that offer full business credit monitoring for all business credit agencies. This means that to view your business credit reports with each business credit agency, you'll likely need to purchase a report with each agency independently.

Check out this business credit monitoring platform: NAV.com

When your business creditors report your payment history, they're reporting the business name, address, and payment data. This means that if you use multiple variations of your business name or business address, you could have separate business credit reports with each agency. For example, if you use "XYZ Construction Inc" with your lumber supplier, but you use "XYZ Inc" with your office supply store, you'll have two separate business credit reports because the business name you used with each company is different. In this instance, you'll want to contact the business credit reporting agency to merge multiple reports.

As you use the same information on all business credit accounts entity documents, licenses, etc., your payment data will match up and build a single business credit report.

The Big 3 Business Credit Reports

Dun & Bradstreet, Experian, and Equifax are the "big three" business credit bureaus that generate business credit reports. These credit reports are created automatically as your business creditors report information about your business. Therefore, when you are applying for business credit with a creditor, it is important that you select creditors that report your business credit. Most lenders or creditors check business credit, but many do not report payment history back to all 3 business credit bureaus. Some creditors only report negative payment history.

Each commercial credit bureau looks at the information they gather in a slightly different way, which can make understanding business credit reports a bit confusing. Here's what you need to know about the business credit bureaus, the information they collect, and the ways it affects your business.

Chapter 3. Dun & Bradstreet (D&B)

Of the "big three" credit bureaus, D&B is the only credit bureau that focuses exclusively on business credit. They report primarily on how a business interacts with vendors and other suppliers, which is why potential suppliers often look at your D&B reports before they offer your business trade credit. In addition to business-to-business data submitted by suppliers, D&B also looks at public records, industry data, and other historical data in your D&B profile to compile their credit scores. The PAYDEX Score is the best-known.

The 100-point PAYDEX score reflects how reliably you've paid your bills and kept your financial obligations to vendors and suppliers that report to D&B. Unfortunately, if you are currently with suppliers who don't report to D&B, that information won't be included when they are calculating your PAYDEX score. Because the PAYDEX score is so important, you should encourage current vendors that don't report your credit history to D&B to do so, or switch to vendors who do report.

Other D&B business credit scores include:
Delinquency Predictor Score: This score measures whether a business is likely to pay their bills late or go bankrupt over

the next 12 months.

Failure Score: This score is designed to predict the possibility that a company will seek legal relief from creditors or go out of business and leave creditors unpaid in the next 12 months.

Supplier Evaluation Risk Rating: This rating predicts the likelihood that a business might stop delivering its goods and services over the next 12 months.

D&B Rating: This rating relies upon company financial statements and other public information to develop an overall rating for a business's credit worthiness. Making sure that your D&B profile includes accurate, up-to-date financial statements can improve your D&B rating greatly.

Credit Limit Recommendation: Banks and creditors may look at this recommendation, which is based on a business's size, industry, and payment history.

HOW TO APPLY FOR YOUR FREE DUNS NUMBER WITH D&B:

- **Follow this link:**
  https://www.dnb.com/duns-number/get-a-duns.html

- **Click the drop down on the primary reason for D-U-N-S Number and choose what best applies for your business.**

- Then, fill up all the form most especially those with asterisk. You do not need to fill out those fields without an asterisk because that information is not required.

- Submit the form.

- It will give you a search result. If you do not find your business in the search result, click "Get D-U-N-S Number" at the bottom of the search list.

- It will route you to a page where there are three options you can choose.

- Choose and click the "Get Started" button at the bottom of the first box which is D-U- N-S Number + Credit Signal– Free.

- Put in your first name, last name, and email.
- Select the "I agree to the Product License Agreement and Privacy Policy Box," then click

- "Register."

- You will receive an email for a temporary password.

- Manually type in the temporary password they provided (which is on the email just sent you) in the password section on the D&B page, then click "log in."

- It will ask you to change your password.

- To change your password, type in the temporary password they gave you and put in your new password. Confirm it by retyping your new password.

- Then, click update.

- Once updated, it will route you to the Company Information Form.

- Fill up the fields with the asterisk. It is okay not to put information on the field without asterisks because those fields are not required.

- You don't necessarily need to select the promotional boxes at the bottom of the form for Legal Zoom and ADP subscriptions. It will be up to you if you really need those options.

- Once you are done filling it out, you can click submit.

After submission you will be routed to a page confirming that you have submitted a request successfully, and you will get your DUNS number within 2 to 4 weeks.

A representative from D & B likely will call you to offer and sell their various services. Please consult with your team before making any purchases directly with D&B. Typically, we don't recommend additional purchases with D&B no matter how urgent they make it sound. Business credit bureaus don't operate like personal credit bureaus and don't follow the same regulations.

Updating D&B

You can update your own business information with D&B by logging into your purchased monitoring account or the free update account. Once you are logged in, edit your business information. Some factors can't be adjusted like your incorporation date, officers, or financial data. To edit these items, you will need to call or email D&B directly. Be aware that you may need to furnish supporting documentation. If the documents don't support the changes you have proposed, your information won't be updated.

Special note: D&B can red flag accounts if they feel the business is trying to set up a business credit report dishonestly. All information that you submit should be factual.

Chapter 4. Equifax

Equifax transforms data collected by the Small Business Finance Exchange (SBFE) into a report. The SBFE is an association of U.S. small business lenders who report payment data on their small business customers. Because this data directly reflects how small businesses interact with lenders, banks use it to evaluate your credit worthiness.

Like the other business credit bureaus, Equifax also uses trade credit information and data from the public record, such as liens, bankruptcies, or judgements against a business to compile a company's credit report.

Equifax credit reports include:

Payment Trend and Payment Index: This shows the business's payment trends over the past 12 months and compares to industry norms.

Equifax Business Credit Risk Score: This predicts the likelihood of a business incurring a 90-day severe delinquency or charge-off over the next 12 months. The score ranges from 101 to 992; lower scores indicate a higher risk.

Equifax Business Failure Score: This predicts the likelihood of a business failing through either formal or informal bankruptcy over the next 12 months. The score ranges from 1000to 1610; lower scores indicate a higher risk.

Updating Equifax

Business Equifax will ask that you update your information through your creditors. After multiple billing cycles, if the errors aren't corrected, you also can try to contact their customer service group.

For more info, visit:
https://www.equifax.com/business/

Chapter 5. Experian

Experian collects credit information from suppliers and lenders. They also look at information available in the public record including legal filings from local, county, and state governments, as well as information from credit card companies, collection agencies, corporate financial information, and other databases.

Experian gathers a lot of data from banks too. They look at the number of credit transactions and outstanding balances a business has. They analyze payment habits, available credit, and the details of any current liens, judgments, or bankruptcies. Time in business, the size of your business, and your business's Standard Industry Classification (SIC) codes are also part of your Experian Business Credit Score.

This score ranges from 0 to 100 and breaks down as follows:
- 0-15: High Risk
- 16-30: Medium Risk
- 31-80: Good Credit
- 80-100: Excellent Credit

Experian also generates a Financial Stability Risk Rating that measures the risk of a company going into bankruptcy or severe financial distress in the next 12 months. This rating ranges from 1 to 5, with lower ratings indicating a lower risk. Because Experian collects both trade data and bank data, their business credit report could be considered the most balanced of the "big three." Whether you rely primarily on trade credit for capital, access capital from a bank, or both, Experian will have data on your business.

Updating Experian

You can update your information with Business Experian by going to www.businesscreditfacts.com.
You may be asked to verify yourself as an individual authorized to make the changes.
For more info:
https://www.experian.com/small-business/establish-business-credit

FUNDING

Obtaining Credit from Banks

- Banks and credit unions allow you to obtain lines of credit to obtain funding.
- Applying for Credit Cards
- You open 6 different windows on your computer and apply for all the credit cards at the same time.
- You are applying for 6 different cards at the same time, but you are applying for Alliant first.
- Delete the inquiries from your credit report before you apply so the banks won't deny you even if you have open accounts.
- When you apply for credit cards, they rely on the income that you state that you make.
- Put a higher income on your application. Be mindful your tax information can be requested.
- At minimum, you should have $25,000 worth of credit from your inquiries.
- At maximum, you should have $50,000-$60,000 worth of credit from your inquiries.
- It is important to know what your credit profile is with Equifax, TransUnion, and Experian.
- It is important to know which banks pull from a particular credit bureau so that you know what cards you should apply to get.
- You want all of your credit profiles to be strong with the credit bureaus, but if you have a report that is weak with one bureau, don't apply for a card that pulls from that bureau so that it will not affect your approval.
- Alliant Credit Union - Preferred Lender
- You have to apply to become a member with them.
- They have a 2% Visa Signature Rewards Program that

gives you 2% back on whatever you spend.

- If you make a donation to Alliant Credit Union, you can get access to them.
- They give $15,000-$25,000 for people with mediocre or medium-build credit.
- Use Alliant to help build your credit once you get established.
- Open a checking account and then apply to open a credit card.
- They closely examine credit inquiries, so apply with them first.
- They are the strictest on credit inquiries.
- Alliant primarily utilizes Equifax.
- Barclays Card
- They have an Aviator Card which grants a free companion pass for a year when you spend over $25,000 dollars.
- You can earn a free companion pass for one trip when you spend $3,000-$4,000.
- It is connected to American Airlines.
- You can apply for one credit card per day. Barclays primarily uses TransUnion.
- They closely examine credit inquiries however not much as Alliant Credit Union, so apply second.

Bank of America

- Business Advantage Travel Card or Bank of America Advantage Card
- 2-3-4 Rule - You can get 2 cards every 2 months,
- 3 cards every 12 months, and 4 cards every 24 months.
- Their rules only apply to cards with Bank of America. They are not judging if you have applied for cards with other banks.
- You can acquire 2 cards. They primarily use Experian.
- If you apply for the Business Advantage Travel Card and Advantage Cash Card, you can attain 2 credit cards with 1 inquiry with Experian.
- They do not examine credit inquiries as closely as Alliant and Barclays, therefore apply third.

- ## Capital One
  - The Savor One card has allied many people to get a credit limit of $30,000.
  - Capital One pulls your credit report from all 3 credit bureaus.

- ## Navy Federal CreditUnion
  - It gives high credit limits to people who are accepted into their creditUnion.
  - You have to be a member or a family member of someone in the military to be accepted.
  - There are ways around the military requirement to join their creditUnion.
  - You can join their creditUnion with someone if you are a

roommate or a family member in the military.

- You can say that you have a grandparent who was in the military who passed away.
- They may ask for that person's information, and you can say that you do not have that information.
- I have seen 80-90% of people who use this method get approved with the creditUnion.
- Don't apply for a credit card as soon as you open an account.
- Allow your account to remain open for 30 days and build a relationship with the bank before applying for credit.
- This relationship with the bank will help you acquire a higher credit limit when you apply for a credit card.
- Set up direct deposit with the bank if you can and you get an additional $15,000 in funding.
- Do not give someone your membership code because if they do something fraudulent, they can have your membership revoked.
- Navy Federal Credit Union may pull from Equifax or TransUnion.

Secured Loans

- I do not recommend secured credit cards.
- You should apply for a secured loan 3 times so you have 3 positive accounts in good standing.
- You have 3 payments each month in good standing.
- Put $1000 in a savings account, and when it is released,

put it in another bank.
- You keep repeating the process.
- You should pay the minimum amount each month for 6-9 months to build your credit report and help your credit score grow 6 points for each positive account.
- Use smaller banks like PNC or Regions or local banks depending on where you live.
- Smaller banks typically offer better programs for secure loans.
- Call your local banks and ask about secure loans.

Websites to help you build your credit

- www.creditbuildercard.com
- www.SelfLender.com
- www.myjewelryclub.com
- www.fingerhut.com
- www.gettingtons.com
- www.rentalkarma.com
- www.oxpublishing.com
- www.vitalcard.com
- www.huttonchase.com
- www.crownjewelers.com

Travel - Perks and Benefits

- Many companies such as Delta partner with other companies and offer affiliate fees which give us discounts

on industries such as travel and vehicles.
- These companies have online shopping portals that allow you to earn flight miles if you shop with another partner vendor like Macys.
  - Use the United Shopping Portal to help you earn points that you can use with credit cards companies.
- Airlines like Delta or United, allow you to earn points that you can redeem for flights perks like upgraded seats for first class seats.
- When you create an online shopping portal profile, you can shop for $4,000-$5,000 in merchandise at Macys that you redeem for flight points with airlines like Delta and United.
- When you purchase your free ticket or upgrade your seats for your flight using the points that the airlines give you for your shopping, you will have earned travel rewards just for using your card to purchase merchandise in a store.
- You should have 2-3 inquiries on your credit report.
- You should have zero derogatory reports including no collection accounts.
- These are the data points that banks use to judge out credit worthiness.
- It is important to learn for yourself how companies are allowing people to earn higher credit limits.
- You need to learn how you can take advantage of the same credit perks that other people are receiving.
- Things in credit change all the time, and I want you to be

as knowledge able about trends in the credit industry as possible.

- These websites include the information that I study to prepare you to help you manage and repair your credit.
- Doctor of Credit - A company providing credit information and credit card deals to consumers.
- Credit Boards - A website where you can go and learn what steps person stake when filing disputes with creditors.
- You can study what people are doing to settle disputes.
- You can see the disputes and learn who is doing what.
- You can learn what credit cards are giving people higher credit card limits and who is getting approved for those higher limits.
- We can also connect you with one of our Credit Restoration Partners should you need help with your Personal Credit.

If you may be interested in our Done for You Business Credit and Funding Service, visit us at:

Premier1BusinessCredit.com

The Funding Program Cheat Sheet provides a brief overview of funding program groups available to customers through the Business Finance Suite and Direct Funding program. Funding qualification is based on having one "C" of Cash flow, good personal Credit from the customer or a guarantor, or Collateral. If you or your customer has one of these "C" s, there's a good possibility you may qualify for a business loan or line of credit. This cheat sheet includes details on funding programs, rates and terms, important details, and deal submission requirements.

Unsecured Credit Lines/ Cards

Collateral Required	Strong personal credit
Line Amounts	$10,000-$150,000
Term	Revolving credit cards
Rates	0% APR typically for 6-18 months, after that 5-29% APR,.8-12% success rate fee paid after funded
Credit Requirements	Excellent personal credit required with 700 or higher credit score, no late payments or derogatory credit within the last 12 months can be on personal credit now, no open collections or bankruptcies, less than 3 inquiries in the last 6 months on consumer credit report.
Details:	Approval amounts are typically 5 times the amount of their existing highest seasoned limit credit card, must ha1ve open credit cards with balances below 40% of their card limits.
Deal Submission requirements:	Application, credit monitoring login credentials

Business Revenue Lending

Collateral Required	Consistent revenue verifiable through bank statements.
Loan Amounts	$5,000-$500,000
Term	3-36 months
Factor	1.10-1.45%
Credit Requirements	500 credit score or higher, no recent bankruptcies
Details:	Business must earn annual revenue of $120,000 or more per year, must be in business for a year or more, business must do over 5 small transactions each month, financial services industries are prohibited, damaged credit is acceptable.
Deal Submission requirements:	Application, 6 months business bank statements

Merchant Advance	
Collateral Required	Credit card sales
Loan Amounts	$1,000-$500,000
Term	3–18-month term, revolving line-of-credit also available
Rates	10-45%
Credit Requirements	500 credit score or higher
Details:	Business must bring in $100,000 or more per year in credit card sales, typical approval amounts equal to one month's credit card processing volume
Deal Submission requirements:	Application, 3-6 months bank and merchant statements

Account Receivable Financing	
Collateral Required	Account receivables
Loan Amounts	$5,000-$20 million
Term	Up to 80% of receivables can be advanced within 24 hours, 20% minus lender's fee is released once actual invoice is paid.
Rates	1.25-3% discount
Credit Requirements	No credit score requirements to qualify
Details:	Receivables must come from another business or government agency not an individual, business must be open for at least 1 year to qualify, medical receivables can qualify along with construction and conventional receivables
Deal Submission requirements:	Application, breakdown of existing receivables, sample invoke.

Private Equity	
Collateral Required	20% of loan amount required as collateral
Loan Amounts	$150,000-$100 million
Term	2 months to 30 years

Rates	8-18%
Credit Requirements	650 FICO scores or higher
Details:	Loans and credit lines available
Deal Submission requirements:	Application, 2 years personal business tax returns, personal credit report, balance sheet, debt schedule

Equipment-Sale Leaseback

Collateral Required	Existing equipment, or new equipment business wants to purchase Loan Amounts
Loan Amounts	$10,000-$20 million
Term	12-48 months
Rates	7%-28%
Credit Requirements	650 or higher FICO score
Details:	Brand new businesses can qualify, m1mmum down payment may include first and last: months' payments.
Deal Submission requirements:	Application, details on equipment being financed (Depending on loan amount and risk factors, 2 years corp and personal tax returns may be required.)

Equipment Leasing

Collateral Required	Existing equipment, or new equipment business wants to purchase
Loan Amounts	$10,000-$2 million
Term	12-48 months
Rates	7%-28%
Credit Requirements	650 or higher FICO score
Details:	2 years time-in-business required
Deal Submission requirements:	Application, details on equipment being financed

Retirement Account Financing	
Collateral Required	Previous 401K or IRA
Loan Amounts	Up to 100% of current retirement account value that's "rollable" from current employer.
Term	5 years (If applicable)
Rates	5.25% (Prime+ 2) + $1995 rolled in lender fee. (If applicable)
Credit Requirements	None
Details:	No penalties for account roll-over
Deal Submission requirements:	Copy of relevant retirement account statement

Securities Financing	
Collateral Required	Stocks, bonds
Loan Amounts	up to 90% of value of stock or bonds
Term	Line-of-credit
Rates	2-5%
Credit Requirements	No credit requirements
Details:	Most stocks and securities accepted, $250,000 in securities required for approval.
Deal Submission requirements:	Application, copy of securities statement

Inventory Financing	
Collateral Required	Inventory
Loan Amounts	$500,000-$2,000,000
Term	Revolving line-of-credit
Rates	2-21%
Credit Requirements	No credit requirements
Details:	Must have $1,000,000 or more in warehoused inventory to qualify, loan amounts as high as 50% of inventory
Deal Submission requirements:	Application, list of inventory, current value breakdown

Purchase Order Financing	
Collateral Required	Purchase Orders
Loan Amounts	$5,000-$25,0,00
Term	Up to 95% of purchase order can be advanced, 5% less fee is released once actual involce is paid
Rates	1-4%
Credit Requirements	No credit score requirements to qualify
Details:	A business can obtain a Jetter-of-credit for up to 95% of the order, cannot be for unfinished goods
Deal Submission requirements:	Application, copy of purchase order

Enterprise SBA Loans	
Collateral Required	Collateral must be 50% of loan amount
Loan Amounts	$200,000-$12 million
Term	10-25 years
Rates	2-2.75% + prime rate, 3-5 lender points
Credit Requirements	620 FICO scores or higher, no BK in the last 4 years
Details:	For profit companies only, positive trends in sales growth, financials required for qualification, SBA 504 and 7a programs available, can be used for working capital or real estate purchase.
Deal Submission requirements:	Application, 2 years business tax returns, resume, business plan, current P&L, 4 months business bank statements.

Commercial Real Estate Financing	
Collateral Required	Commercial real estate
Loan Amounts	$75,000- 20,000,000
Term	Up to 75% loan-to-value for refinances, up to 90% loan-to-value for purchases, 20-30 year loans
Rates	4-8%

Credit Requirements	650 FICO score
Details:	Conventional, SBA 504 available,
Deal Submission requirements:	Application, 2 years business tax returns, appraisal YTD POL, current debt schedule

Book of Business Financing

Collateral Required	Book of Business
Loan Amounts	Borrow 1.5 time annual renewal
Term	3-10 year loan
Rates	4-16.99% + prime rate
Credit Requirements	620 FICO or higher
Details:	Only available for insurance agents
Deal Submission requirements:	Application, summary of existing renewables

Alternative SBA Loans and Credit Lines

Collateral Required	Unsecured
Loan Amounts	25,000- 5 million
Term	Revolving Line of Credit or 3-5 year term loan
Rates	6% to 21%
Credit Requirements	700+ Fico Scores
Details:	Good personal credit and tax returns with net profits required
Deal Submission requirements:	2 years Business tax returns. Year-to-date Profit and Loss statement, balance sheet, debt schedule, credit monitoring login credentials

Tier I Vendors

Start building your business credit by adding trade accounts.

Add 3 trade accounts from Tier I.

When you make a purchase, do it on your net /credit terms. It is payments on net/credit terms that are reported.

To ensure that your vendors report your payments, make a purchase of $50 or more.

It typically takes 30-90 days for your payments to report on your business credit reports.

Tier I Vendors

76

Phone: 855-241-1818

Website: https://www.76fleet.com

Reports to: D&B, Experian and Equifax

Description:
76 has been on the driver's side for more than 80 years now. The brand's history traces its original company roots all the way back. to Santa Paula, California and Lyman Stewart, a co-founder of Union Oil Company of California. Today 76 is owned by Phillips 66 Company providing you with TOP TIER''' gas in more than 1,800 retail fuel sites in the United States, a1nd giving you its trademark customer service from day one.

Special instruction:

Please keep in mind, before applying ·for multiple accounts with WEX Fleet cards, please make sure to have enough time in between applying so that they don't read flagged your account for fraud.

To Qualify:
-Entity in, good standing with Secretary of State
-EIN number with IRS
-Business address- matching everywhere.
-D&B number
-Business License- if applicable
-Business Bank account
-Business Phone Number Listed in 411
-SSN is required for informational purposes. If concerned they will pull your personal credit please talk to their credit department before applying.
-If not approved based on business credit history or been in business less than 1 year, then a $500 deposit is needed or a Personal Guarantee (PG)
-Can be used at any P66, 76, or Conoco fueling location.

To Apply: Online or over the phone

Terms: Net 15

Advanced Auto Parts

Phone: 877-280-5965

Website: https://shop.advanceautoparts.com/

Reports to: D&B

Description:
Advance Auto Parts, Inc. is a leading automotive aftermarket parts provider that serves both professional installer and do-it-yourself customers. As of October 6, 2018, Advance operated 4,981 stores and 139 Worldpac branches in the United States, Canada, Puerto Rico, and the U.S. Virgin Islands. The Company also serves 1,229 independently owned Carquest branded stores across these locations in addition to Mexico, the Bahamas, Turks and Caicos, British Virgin Islands and Pacific Islands. Additional information about Advance, including employment opportunities, customer services; and online shopping for parts, accessories and other offerings can be found at www.AdvanceAutoParts.com.

To Qualify:
-Entity in good standing with Secretary of State
-EINI number with IRS
-Business address- matching everywhere.
-D&B number
-Business License- if applicable
-Business Bank account
-Initial limit $1000

To Apply· At the branch

Terms: Net 7 or Net 30

Tier I Vendors

Flying J

Phone: 865-474-2953

Website: https://www.pilotflyingj.com

Reports to: D&B

Description:
With over 60 years in business, Flying J is one of the leading gas station or company in the country.

To Qualify:
-Entity in good standing with Secretary of State
-EIN number with IRS
-Business address- matching everywhere.
-D&B number
-Business License- if applicable
-Business Bank account
-Bank reference
-Truckers and Diesel accounts require DOT Registration
-If you don't have an active DOT, they will ask for a lease agreement from the company you possibly lease to.
-Axle, fuel credit card can be used at Pilot and Flying J locations, locations within the One9 Fuel Network, and Pilot Flying J Truck Care locations. One of the benefits of the Axle card is you can use it at over 900 locations nationwide!

To Apply: Online

Terms: Net 7

Tier I Vendors

Global Voice Direct

Phone: 877-308-5803

Website: https://globalvoicedirect.com/

Reports to: Experian and Credit Safe

Description:
AU-Inclusive Cloud Phone System with Voice, fax, SMS & HD Meetings,
Business credit line, business tradeline, start-up vendor account, Conferencing.
audio.

Special Note:
This company's normal turnaround time is 24 hours or greater due to volume.

To Qualify:
-Entity in good standing with Secretary of State
-EIN number with IRS
-Business address- matching everywhere.
-D&B number
-Business License- if applicable
-Business Bank account
-Annual membership of $149 upon application

To Apply: Online

Terms Net 30

Grainger Industrial Supply

Phone: 800-472-4643

Website: https://www.grainger.com/

Reports to: D&B

Description:
Grainger works with more than 11,300 suppliers to provide customers with electrical, fasteners, fleet maintenance, HVACR, hardware, janitorial, material handling, pneumatics, power tools, pumps, and much more.

To Qualify:
-Entity in good standing with Secretary of State
-EIN number with I RS
-Business address- matching everywhere.
-D&B number
-Business License- if applicable
-Business Bank account
-Business registered to Secretary of State (SOS) for at least 60 days old.
-If a business doesn't have an established credit, they will require additional documents like accounts payable, income statement, balance sheets, etc.

Apply: Online or over the phone

Terms: Net 30, Net 45, Net 60 or Net 90

Hardware Express

Phone: 800-335-9072, (Credit Dept. selection number 2)

Website: https://www.e-hardwareexpress.com

Reports to: Experian

Description:
Hardware Express is positioned as the fill-in supplier in a $300 billion industry that includes hardware retailers, home centers, and building supply and mobile home retailers. Our value propulsion focuses on "just in time" inventory and daily delivery on high-velocity items, while differentiating ourselves from other national hardware distributors through competitive pricing without membership, break pack, or miscellaneous fees. We also provide a substantial private label product offering1 allowing for enhanced margins for retailers.

Special Note:

Barnett, Hardware Express, Supply Works, and Wilmar are one entity, each offering different products. Please only apply for one of these four accounts.

Unfortunately, virtual addresses are not accepted.

To Qualify:
-Entity in good standing with Secretary of State
-EIN number with IRS
-Business address- matching everywhere
-D&B number
-Business License- if acceptable
-Business Bank account
-Trade/Bank references
-No minimum time in business
-Virtual addresses are not accepted

To Apply: Over the phone at 888-803-4469

Terms: Net 30

HD Supply

Phone: 800-798-8809

Website: http://www.hdsupply.com/

Reports to: Equifax

Description:
Has a huge selection of tools and materials. It ranges from hand tools, power tools, concrete products and accessories, rebar fabrication, fasteners, connectors, erosion control materials, pipes and fittings, waterproofing needs, drywall accessories and everything to keep your crews safe. You'll also find tool repair service or rental forms, braces, hardware and decorative stamps at many locations.

To Qualify:
-Entity in good standing with Secretary of State
-EIN number with IRS
-Business address- matching everywhere.
-D&B number
-Business License- if applicable
-Business Bank account
-Bank reference
-At least 1 year in credit reporting

To Apply: Online

Terms Net 30

KUM&GO

Phone: 800-517-7556

Website: https://www.kumandgofleet.com/

Reports to: D&B, Experian and Equifax

Description:

In 1959, William A. Krause and Tony S. Gentle created a convenience store concept where people could buy gas & groceries. But more than that, they pioneered a belief system. Whether it's keeping the store sparkling clean, treating every customer like a friend, or donating our time and money to great causes, we strive to make every day just: a little bit better and brighter for all.

Special instruction:

Please keep in mind, before applying for multiple accounts with WEX Fleet cards, please make sure to have enough time in between applying so that they don't red-flagged your account for fraud.

To Qualify:
-Entity in good standing with Secretary of State
-EIN number with IRS
-Business address- matching everywhere.
-D&B number
-Business License- if applicable
-Business Bank account
-Business Phone Number Listed in 411
-SSN is required for informational purposes. If concerned they will pull your personal credit please talk to their credit department before applying.
-If not approved based on business credit history or been in business less than 1 year, then a $500 deposit is needed or a Personal Guarantee (PG)

To Apply: Online or over the phone

Terms: Net 15

Tier I Vendors

Marathon

Phone: 866-562-1045

Website: https://www.marathonbrand.com

Reports to: D&B, Experian and Equifax

Description:
Marathon Petroleum Company LP's (MPCs) marketing organization is recognized as a consistent leader in the petroleum industry. MPC provides transportation fuels, asphalt, and specialty products throughout the United States. Our comprehensive product line supports commercial, industrial, and retail operations.

Special Instruction:

Please keep in mind, before applying for multiple accounts with WEX Fleet cards, please make sure to have enough time in between applying so that they don't red-flagged your account for fraud.

To Qualify:
-Entity in good standing with Secretary of State
-EIN number with IRS
-Business address- matching everywhere.
-D&B number
-Business License- if applicable
-Business Bank account
-Business Phone Number Listed in 411
-SSN is required for informational purposes. If concerned they will pull your personal credit please talk to their credit department before applying.
-If not approved based on business credit history or been in business less than 1 year, then a $500 deposit is needed or a Personal Guarantee, (PG)

To Apply: Online or over the phone

Terms: Net 15

MURPHY USA

Phone: 800-950-6128

Website: https://www.murphyusafleet.com/

Reports to: D&B, Experian and Equifax

Description:
Headquartered in El Dorado, Murphy USA opened its first store in Chattanooga, Tenn., in December 1996. Today, Murphy USA operates more than 1,400 stores in 27 states and employs more than 10,000 people. The stores provide quality, low-priced fuels, and outstanding service to nearly 2 million customers every day to get them where they need to go.

Special instruction:

Please keep in mind, before applying for multiple accounts with WEX Fleet cards, please make sure to have enough time in between applying so that they don't red-flagged your account for fraud.

To Qualify:
-Entity in good standing with Secretary of State
-EIN number with IRS
-Business address- matching everywhere.
-D&B number
-Business License- if applicable
-Business Bank account
-Business Phone Number Listed in 411
-SSN is required for informational purposes. If concerned they will pull your personal credit please talk to their credit department before applying.
-If not approved based on business credit history or been in business less than 1 year, then a $500 deposit is needed or a Personal Guarantee (PG)

To Apply: Online or over the phone

Terms: Net 15

Supply Works

Phone: 888-820-6515 (Credit Dept selection number 2)

Website: https://www.supplyworks.com

Reports to: Experian

Description:
Home Depot Pro, formerly SupplyWorks, powers pros to get more done. We are your single-source supplier for facilities maintenance supplies, including everything from cleaning and janitorial supplies and PPE to plumbing parts and lighting products.

Special Note:

Barnett, Hardware Express, Supply Works, and Wilmar are one entity, each offering different products. Please only apply for one of these 4 accounts.

Unfortunately, virtual addresses are not accepted.

To Qualify:
-Entity in good standing with Secretary of State
-EIN number with IRS
-Business address- matching everywhere.
-D&B number
-Business License- if applicable
-Business Bank account
-Trade/Bank references
-No minimum time in business

To Apply: Online or over the phone.

Terms: Net 30

Tier I Vendors

ULINE
Phone: 800-295-5510

Website: https://www.uline.com

Reports to: D&B and Experian

Description:
Uline is the leading distributor of Shipping, Industrial, and Packing materials,
Industrial and Janitorial Products. 99.5% of Uline's orders! hip the same day, with
no back orders.

To Qualify:
-Entity in good standing with Secretary of State
-EIN number with IRS
-Business address- matching everywhere.
-D&B number
-Business License- if applicable
-Business Bank account
-Business Phone Number Listed in 411
-Application may be approved for net 30 at time of order. Upon final review,
Credit Department may change to a few pre paid orders, before a Net 30 is
granted

To Apply:

Will need to create an account first, then place an order and select Net 30 terms.
Credit dept. will review the account.

Terms: Net 30

Tier I Vendors

WEX Fleet

Phone: 800-395-0812 option 3

Website: https://www.wexinc.com/solutions/fleet-management/

Reports to: D&B, Experian and Equifax

Description:
Wrights Express (WEX Card) offers universal fleet cards, heavy truck cards, and universally accepted business fleet cards designed with features that support the small business, including a rewards program.

Special instruction:
Please keep in mind, before applying for multiple accounts with WEX Fleet cards, please make sure to have enough time in between applying so that they don't red-flagged your account for fraud.

To Qualify:
-Entity in good standing with Secretary of State
-EIN number with IRS
-Business address- matching everywhere.
-D&B number
-Business License- if applicable
-Business Bank account
-Business Phone Number Listed in 411
-SSN is required for informational purposes. If concerned they will pull your personal credit please talk to their credit department before applying.
-If not approved based on business credit history or been in business less than 1 year, then a $500 deposit is needed or a Personal Guarantee (PG)

To Apply: Online or Over the phone

Terms: Net 15 (WEX Fleet Card), Net 26, or Revolving (WEX FlexCard)

Wilmar

Phone: 888-803-4470

Website: https://www.wilmar.com/

Reports to: Experian

Description:
At Wilmar, we're bringing you more of what you need to stay ahead in a highly competitive industry: more products, more convenience, and more services. Now part of The Home Depot family of quality brands, we are the nation's largest distributor of maintenance supplies excursively for apartment housing with a dedicated focus on providing quality products and proven solutions to improve your property performance.

Special Note:

Barnett, Hardware Express, Supply Works and Wilmar are one entity, each offering different products. Please only apply for one of these 4 accounts.

Unfortunately, virtual addresses are not accepted.

To Qualify:
-Entity in good standing with Secretary of State
-EIN number with IRS
-Business address- matching everywhere.
-D&B number
-Business License- if applicable
-Business Bank account
-Trade/Bank references
-No minimum time in business

To Apply: Online-need to fill-up the credit application form and send that Via email:customercarre@wilmarr.com or Fax: 800.436.9192

Terms Net 30

Tier II Vendors

You currently should have 3 trade accounts reporting to your business credit reports.

Now, add 3 more accounts from Tier II.

When you make a purchase, do so on your net/credit terms. It is payments on net/credit terms that are reported.

To ensure that your vendors report your payments, make a purchase of $50 or more.

It typically takes 30-90 days for your payments to report on your business credit reports.

Tier II Vendors

7-Eleven

Phone: 866-910-7991

Website: https://www.7-eleven.com/

Reports to: D&B, Experian and Equifax

Description:
The more you fuel at 7-Eleven, the more you save-up to 7 off per gallon on any fuel brand at our pumps!

Special Instruction:
Please keep in mind, before applying for multiple accounts with 'WEX Fleet cards, please make sure to have enough time in between applying so that they don't red-flagged your account for fraud.

To Qualify:
-Entity in good standing with Secretary of State
-EIN number with IRS
-Business address- matching everywhere.
-D&B number
-Business License- if applicable
-Business Bank account
-Business Phone Number Listed in 411
-Established business credit history
-At least 1 year in business
-If less than 1 year in business will need a PG. Can give a 500 deposit instead of using a PG.

To Apply; Online

Terms: Net 15

Amazon

Phone: 866-634-8381

Website: https://www.amazon.com

Reports to: D&B and Equifax

Description:
Online shopping, from the earth's biggest selection of books, magazines, music, DVDs, videos, electronics, computers, software, apparel & accessories, shoes, and much more.

To Qualify:
-Entity in good standing with Secretary of State
-EIN number with IRS
-Business address- matching everywhere.
-D&B number
-Business License- if applicable
-Business Bank account
-Business Phone Number Listed in 411
-No minimum time in business if strong business credit history
-Will pull business credit reports to make sure some established business credit history.
-Must have a good D&B paydex score of 80 or higher and a good Equifax business credit score
-The company has been in business for more than 2 years but does not have an established business credit history, a Personal Guarantee (PG) is recommended but not required. It may increase the likelihood of approval and is recommended if you have a young or small business. And not enough business credit history.

To Apply: Online

Terms: Net 55

Creative Analytics

Phone: 202-688-3932

Website: https://creativeanalyticsdc.com/

Reports to: Equifax and Credit Safe

Description:
A digital marketing agency and management consulting firm, Creative Analytics offers office products such as small electronics, desk and office decor/accessories, fitness items, beauty professional tools, kitchen items, etc. as well as monthly digital marketing services (e.g. websites and social media plans).

Special instructions:

Account holders with monthly subscriptions get monthly revolving accounts with credit lines of up to $10,000 reported. There is a $79 fee to apply (refunded if denied based on criteria below), and $100 minimum purchase to be reported. The annual fee counts toward that minimum.

To Qualify:
-Entity in good standing with Secretary of State
-Business credit history
-EIN number with IRS
-Business address- matching everywhere.
-D&B Number
-Business License- if applicable
-Business Bank account
-Established business for at least 30 days
-Must have a good D&B paydex score of 80 or higher
-Has a yearly membership fee of $79

To Apply: Online

Terms: Net 30

CDW

Phone: 800-800-4239 option 4

Website: https://www.cdw.com/

Reports to: D&B

Description:
CDW is a leading multi-brand technology solutions provider to business, government, education, and healthcare organizations in the United States, the United Kingdom, and Canada. A Fortune 500 company with multi-national capabilities. Our broad array of offerings range from hardware and software to integrated IT solutions such as security, cloud, data center, and networking.

To Qualify:
-Entity in good standing with Secretary of State
-EIN number with IRS
-Business address- matching everywhere.
-D&B number
-Business License- if applicable
-Business Bank account
-Must have a good D&B paydex score of 80 or higher
-At least 2 years in the business

To Apply: Over the phone

Terms Net 30

Tier II Vendors

Digi-Key

Phone: 800-338-4105

Website: https://www.digikey.com/

Reports to: D&B

Description:
Digi-Key is one of the fastest-growing distributors of electronic components in the world. Founded in 1972, Digi-Key was a pioneer in the mail-order catalog business and a key resource for design engineers. Today Digi-Key offers the world's largest selection of electronic components in stock and available for immediate shipment.

To Qualify:
-Entity in good standing with Secretary of State
-EIN number with IRS
-Business address- matching everywhere
-D&B number
-Business License- if applicable
-Business Bank account
-Trade/credit references
-Must have a good D&B paydex score of 80 or higher
-3 accounts reporting

To Apply: Online

Terms Net 30

Exxon Mobil

Phone: 855-447-1632

Website: http://.exxonmobil.com/

Reports to: D&B and Experian

Description:
ExxonMobil, one of the world's largest publicly traded energy providers and chemical manufacturers, develops and applies next-generation technologies to help safely and responsibly meet the world's growing needs for energy and high quality chemical products.

Special Instruction:
Please keep in mind, before applying for multiple accounts with WEX Fleet cards, please make sure to, have enough time in between applying so that they don't red-flagged your account for fraud

To Qualify:
-Entity in good standing with Secretary of State
-EIN number with IRS
-Business address- matching everywhere.
-D&B number
-Business License- if applicable
-Business Bank account
-At least 1 year in business
-Must have a good D&B paydex score of 80 or higher
-SSN is required for informational purposes. If concerned they will pull your personal credit please talk to their credit department before applying.
-If not approved based on business credit history or been in business less than 1 year, then a $500 deposit is needed or a Personal Guarantee, (PG)

To Apply: Online or Over the Phone

Terms: Net 15

Fleet Pride

Phone: 361-883-4358

Website: https://fleetpride.com/

Reports to: D&B

Description:

FleetPride specializes in selling Parts and providing Services for heavy-duty trucks and trailers, primarily Class 6-8. We serve all vocations and sell to multiple industries, including agriculture, construction, energy, freight and shipping, food and beverage, leasing, long and short haul, mining, transit and school bus, waste management, intermodal and work trucks.

To Qualify:
-Entity in good standing with Secretary of State
-Business credit history
-EIN number with IRS
-Business address- matching everywhere.
-D&B number
-Business License- if applicable
-Business Bank account
-Three (3) trade credit references
-Tax exempt information - if applicable
-No minimum time in business

To Apply· Online

Terms: Net 30

Tier II Vendors

GetGo

Phone: 800-841-1426

Website: https://www.getgotleet.com/

Reports to: D&B, Experian and Equifax

Description:
Whether your fleet operates regionally or drives your business further, GetFleet from GetGo delivers savings and control tools that put fleet managers in the driver's seat!

Special Instruction:

Please keep in mind, before applying for multiple accounts with WEX Fleet cards, please make sure to have enough time in between applying so that they don't red-flagged your account for fraud.

To Qualify:
-Entity in good standing with Secretary of State
-EIN number with IRS
-Business address- matching everywhere.
-D&B number
-Business License- if applicable
-Business Bank account
-Business Phone Number Listed in 411
-SSN is required for informational purposes. If concerned they will pull your personal credit please talk to their credit department before applying.
-If not approved based on business credit history or been in business less than 1 year, then a $500 deposit 1s needed or a Personal Guarantee (PG)

To Apply; Online or over the phone

Terms: Net 15

Global Fleet

Phone: 800-903-5338

Website: https://www.global-fleet.com

Reports to: D&B, Experian and Equifax

Description:
Owned and operated by CSI Enterprises, Inc., Global-Fleet has been a recognized leader in the commercial fleet fuel business for over 30 years, with international customers spanning the Americas, Canada, Europe and Asia. We provide our clients with the most advanced fleet fuel program available, supported by 24/7 customer service.

To Qualify:
Global Fleet
Step 5 (Net 30)
-Entity in good standing with Secretary of State
-EIN number with IRS
-Business address- matching everywhere.
-D&B number
-Business License- if applicable
-Business Bank account
-3 years in business for Global Fleet, Voyager CSI Fleet, and CSI Fleet M/C
-Personal Guarantee (PG) may not be required, based on credit check

Global-Fleet- Flex
Step 7- Flex (Net 30 or Revolving)
-Entity in good standing with Secretary of State
-EIN number with IRS
-Business address- matching everywhere.
-D&B number
-Business License- if applicable
-Business Bank account
-A Personal Guarantee (PG) is required

To Apply: Over the phone

Terms: Net 30 or Revolving

Graybar

Phone: 8.55-347-2839

Website: https://www.graybar.com/store/en/gb

Reports to: D&B - Quarterly

Description:

Graybar is an American employee-owned corporation, based in Clayton, Missouri. It conducts a wholesale distribution business for electrical, communications and data networking products, and is a provider of related supply-chain management and logistics services.

To Qualify:
-Entity in good standing with Secretary of State
-EIN number with IRS
-Business address- matching everywhere.
-D&B Number
-Business License- if applicable
-Business Bank account
-Bank references
-Trade references
-Must have a good D&B paydex score of 80 or higher

To Apply; At the store or online

Terms: Net 30

Tier II Vendors

Gulf Fleet

Phone: 844-688-6867

Website: https://www.gulffleetcard.com/

Reports to: D&B, Experian and Equifax

Description:
Gulf Fleet Fuel Cards outperform cash and regular credit cards. Apply for a
commercial, universal, or business gas card for savings and convenience.

Special Instruction:

Please keep in mind, before applying for multiple accounts with WEX Fleet cards,
please make sure to, have enough time in between applying so that they don't
red-flagged your account for fraud.

To Qualify:
-Entity in good standing with Secretary of State
-EIN number with IRS
-Business address- matching everywhere.
-D&B number
-Business License- if applicable
-Business Bank account
-Business Phone Number Listed in 411
-SSN is required for informational purposes. If concerned they will pull your
person al credit please talk to their credit department before applying.
-If not approved based on business credit history or been in business less than 1
year then a $500 deposit is needed or a Personal Guarantee (PG)

To Apply: Online or over the phone (1-877-516-4097)

Terms: Net 15

Hisco

Phone: 763-657-2810

Website: https://www.hisco.com/

Reports to: D&B - can take up to 2 to 3 months to report from date paid

Description:
Hisco is North America's premier distributor of mission-critical materials. For more than 42 years, Hisco has been a leader in supply chain solutions. Their mission is to be a trusted solutions provider committed to profitable growth through investment, innovation, and operational excellence.

To Qualify:
-Entity in good standing with Secretary of State
-EINI number with IRS
-Business address- matching everywhere.
-D&B number
-Business License- if applicable
-Business Bank account
-Bank reference
-Current Financial Statement
-3 Trade/credit references

To Apply: Over the phone

Terms Net 30

Holiday

Phone: 800-745-7411, ext. 8889 or 8521

Website: https://www.holidayfleetcards.com/

Reports to: D&B, Experian and Equifax

Description:
Holiday is your one-stop-shop for all of your commercial fueling needs! Whether you have one or five hundred vehicles, Holiday Fleet cards can help you manage your business more efficiently. With optional acceptance at more than 90% of fuel retailers nationwide, our fuel cards offer the utmost in convenience for your business.

Special instruction:

Please keep in mind, before applying ·for multiple accounts with WEX Fleet cards, please make sure to have enough time in between applying so that they don't red-flagged your account for fraud.

To Qualify:
-Entity in good standing with Secretary of State
-EIN number with IRS
-Business address- matching everywhere.
-D&B number
-Business License- if applicable
-Business Bank account
-Business Phone Number Listed in 411
-Some established business credit
-Must have a good D&B paydex score of 80 or higher
-SSN is required for informational purposes. If concerned they will pull your personal credit please talk to their credit department before applying.
-If not approved based on business credit history been in business less than 1 year, then a $500 deposit is needed or a Personal Guarantee (PG)

To Apply: Online or over the phone

Terms: Net 25

Home Depot

Website: https://www.homedepot.com

Reports to: D&B, Experian and Equifax

Description:
The Home Depot provides products and services for all your home improvement needs. Their Commercial Revolving Charge Card gives your business payment flexibility and provides a boost to your business credit profile at the same time.

To Qualify:
-Commercial Account (Pay in Full Terms)
-Entity in good standing with Secretary of State
-EIN number with IRS
-Business address- matching everywhere.
-D&B number
-Business License- if applicable
-Business Bank account
-They like to see minimum 2 accounts reporting, but look at merit of overall application
-Must have a minimum of 10 employees
-Business Phone Number Listed in 411
-At least 3 years in the business.
-Can request Net 60 after account is established
-Personal Guarantee (PG) may be required

Commercial Revolving Charge Account
-Entity in good standing with Secretary of State
-EIN number with IRS
-Business address- matching everywhere.
-D&B number
-Business License- if applicable
-Business Bank Account
-Business Phone Number Listed in 411
-No minimum time in business
-A Personal Guarantee (PG) Is required

To Apply: Online or in store

Terns: Net 30, Net 60, Net 90 or Revolving

Industrial fans Direct

Phone: 866-727-1060

Website: https://www.industrialfansdirect.com/pages/net-30-terms-and-payment

Reports to: D&B and Equifax

Description:
Based in Mukilteo, Washington, IndustrialFansDirect.com is your commercial and industrial ventilation, heating and lighting resource. We specialize in working with mechanical contractors, engineers, electricians, facility managers, and commercial building owners to provide high quality air movement and work environment
solutions.

To Qualify:
-Entity in good standing with Secretary of State
-EIN number with IRS
-Business address- matching everywhere.
-D&B number
-Business License- if applicable
-Business Bank account
-Bank reference
-Trade/credit references
-Must have a good Equifax business credit score
-Minimum order of $500

To Apply: Online

Terms: Net 30

Tier II Vendors

Lowe's

Phone:866-855-4429

Website: https://www.lowes.com

Reports to: D&B, Experian and Equifax

Description:
Lowe's is a large retailer of Building and Home Supplies: Tools, Kitchen
Appliances, Cabinets, Hardware, Countertops, and Paint. Purchase online or at
your local Lowe's store.

To Qualify:
Accounts Receivable Card or Business Rewards Card from American Express
-Entity in good standing with Secretary of State
-EIN number with IRS
-Business address- matching everywhere.
-D&B number
-Business License- if applicable
-Business Bank account
-Business Phone Number Listed in 411
-Established business credit history
-No minimum time in business
-Must have a good D&B paydex score of 80 or higher
-Can apply without a PG and credit dept. will review.
-If not approved based on business credit history, then a Personal Guarantee
(PG), is required.

To Apply: Online or at the store

Terms:

Net 30, 60 (Accounts Receivable Card)

Net 25, or Revolving (Business Rewards Card from American Express)

Tier II Vendors

LUKOIL

Phone: 888-737-7626

Website: http://www.lukoil.com/

Reports to: D&B, Experian and Equifax

Description:
LUKOIL is one of the largest publicly traded, vertically integrated oil and gas companies in the world accounting for more than 2% of the world's oil production and around 1% of the proved hydrocarbon reserves. Special Instruction:
Please keep in mind, before applying for multiple accounts with WEX Fleet cards, please make sure to, have enough time in between applying so that they don't red-flagged your account for fraud.

To Qualify:
-Entity in good standing with Secretary of State
-EINI number with IRS
-Business address- matching everywhere.
-D&B number
-Business License- if applicable
-Business Bank account
-Business Phone Number Listed in 411
-SSN is required for informational purposes. If concerned they will pull your person al credit please talk to their credit department before applying.
-If not approved based on business credit history or been in business less than 1 year then a $500 deposit is needed or a Personal Guarantee (PG)

To Apply: Online

Terms: Net 15

Maverick

Phone: 844-379-5893

Website: https://www.wexinc.com/solutions/fleet-cards/select/maverik-fleet-card/

Reports to: D&B, Experian, and Equifax

Description:
Maverik provides two fleet card options to best fit your needs. The Maverik Fleet card lets you fuel at any Maverik locations while providing security, control, and valuable reporting. The Maverik Universal card includes all of the benefits of the Maverik fleet card but can be used at 95% of fueling sites nationwide.

Special Instruction:

Please keep in mind, before applying for multiple accounts with WEX Fleet cards, please make sure to have enough time in between applying so that they don't red-flagged your account for fraud.

To Qualify:
-Entity in good standing with Secretary of State
-EIN number with IRS
-Business address- matching everywhere.
-D&B number
-Business License- if applicable
-Business Bank account
-Business Phone Number Listed in 411
-SSN is required for informational purposes. If concerned they will pull your person- al credit please talk to their credit department before applying.
-If not approved based on business credit history or been in business less than 1 year, then a $500 deposit is needed or a Personal Guarantee, (PG)

To Apply: Online or over the phone

Terms: Net 15

Meijer

Phone: 866-558-5981

Website: https://www.meijer.com

Reports to: D&B, Experian and Equifax

Description:
Over 200 fuel locations to serve you throughout the Midwest in MI, OH, IN, IL, KY, and now in WI. When a Meijer location isn't convenient, the card is accepted at thousands of fuel and service locations nationwide, anywhere WEX Inc. is accepted.

Special Instruction:

Please keep in mind, before applying for multiple accounts with WEX Fleet cards, please make sure to, have enough time in between applying so that they don't red-flag1ged your account for fraud.

To Qualify:
-Entity in good standing with Secretary of State
-EIN number with IRS
-Business address- matching everywhere.
-D&B number
-Business License- if applicable
-Business Bank account
-Business Phone Number Listed in 411
-SSN is required for informational purposes. If concerned they will pull your person al credit please talk to their credit department before applying.
-If not approved based on business credit history or been in business less than 1 year then a $500 deposit is needed or a Personal Guarantee (PG)

To Apply: Online or over the phone

Terms: Net 15

Northern Tool

Phone: 888-321-6698

Reports to: D&B and Experian

Website: https://www.northerntool.com

Description:
Northern Tool+ Equipment is truly a multi-channel retailer offering a wide selection of products - from consumer goods to industrial and construction equipment - to do-it-yourselfers, contractors and professional shops via catalog, internet (northerntool.com), mobile and retail locations.

To Qualify:
-Entity in good standing with Secretary of State
-EIN number with IRS
-Business address- matching everywhere.
-D&B number
-Business License- if applicable
-Business Bank account
-Business Phone Number Listed in 411
-Bank references
-Trade references
-Good Business Experian credit score
-At least .3 years in business
-If not approved based on business credit history or been in business for less than 3 years, they may ask for a Personal Guarantee (PG).

To Apply: Online or at the branch

Terms - Net 30

Office Depot

Phone: 800-767-1358

Website: https://business.officedepot.com

Reports to: D&B, Experian and Equifax

Description:
Office Depot® OfficeMax® is a resource and a catalyst to help customers work better. We are a single source for everything customers need to be more productive, including the latest technology, core office supplies, print and document services., business services, facilities products, furniture, and school essentials.

To Qualify:
Business Account with Full Balance Due Terms (Net 30)
-Entity in good standing with Secretary of State
-EIN number with IRS
-Business address- matching everywhere.
-D&B number
-Business License- if applicable
-Business Bank account
-At least 3 years in business
-Must have a good D&B paydex score of 80 or higher

Business Credit Account (Revolving)
-Entity in good standing with Secretary of State
-EIN number with IRS
-Business address- matching everywhere.
-D&B number
-Business License- if applicable
-Business Bank account
-A corporation with more than $5 million annual sales and in business for at least 3 years

To Apply: Online or at store

Terms: Net 30 or Revolving

Quick Trip

Phone: 888-737-7633

Website: https://www.quiktripfleetoffers.c.om/

Reports to: D&B, Experian and Equifax

Description:
QuikTrip provides a quick fix for those on the go. QuikTrip (QT) owns and operates about 670 gasoline/convenience stores in nearly a dozen states, mostly in the central US. QT stores, which average 4,600 sq. ft., feature the ·company's own QT brand of gas and diesel fuel, as well as brand-name beverages, candy, and tobacco. QT's. 15-plus travel centers offer scales, food, fuel, showers, and other services for truckers. The firm's FleetMaster program offers commercial trucking companies detailed reports showing drivers' product purchases, amounts spent, and odometer readings.

To Qualify:
QT Fleetmaster
-Entity in good standing with Secretary of State
-EIN number with IRS
-Business address- matching everywhere.
-D&B number
-Business License- if applicable
-Business Bank account
-Business Phone Number Listed in 411
-Gross annual revenue
-$500 deposit or a Personal Guarantee (PG) may be required

QT Fleetmaster Plus
-There is a $40 set-up fee for the account and a $2/per month/per card fee for QT Fleetmaster Plus

To Apply: Online or over the phone

Terms: Net 15

QuickCheck

Phone: 866-726--4199

Website: https://quikcheck.com/

Reports to: D&B

Description:
The QuickCheck Universal Fleet Card is accepted at all QuickCheck locations. If you need to fuel outside our area, the card is accepted at over 90% of U.S. retail fuel locations nationwide!

Special Instruction:
Please keep in mind, before applying' for multiple accounts with WEX Fleet cards, please make sure to have enough time in between applying so that they don't red flagged your account for fraud.

To Qualify:
-Entity in good standing with Sectary of State
-EIN number with IRS
-Business address- matching everywhere.
-D&B number
-Business License- if applicable
-Business Bank account
-Business Phone Number Listed in 411
-SSN is required for informational purposes. If concerned they will pull your personal credit please talk to their credit department before applying.
-If not approved based on business credit history or been in business less than 1 year, then a $500 deposit is needed or a Personal Guarantee (PG)

To Apply: Online or over the phone

Terms: Net 15

Tier II Vendors

Quill

Phone: 800-982-3400

Reports to; D&B

Website: https://www.quill.com/

Description:
Quill sells office supplies, cleaning supplies, packing and shipping supplies, school supplies, printing supplies, and more. From filling and storage to hand held computers, Quill has a wide range of discounted top name brand products.

Special Instruction:
If not given a Net .30 they will ask you to do prepaid orders of $100.00. Normally any prepaid order don't report but you would need them to have given you a Net 30 account. Net 30 accounts require $50.00 purchase to report.
**Sometimes an order is shipped, and customer thinks they are approved, and may not be. Takes Credit Department approximately 3 hours to process application

To Qualify:
-Entity in good standing with Secretary of State
-EIN number with IRS
-Business address- matching everywhere.
-D&B number
-Business License- if applicable
-Business Bank account
-New business or businesses with no Credit history may need to pre-pay purchases until Net 30 is approved

To Apply: Online or over the phone

Terms: Net 30

Tier II Vendors

Sheetz

Phone: 888-737-7634

Website: https://www.sheetz.com/

Reports to: D&B, Experian and Equifax

Description:
Use your card at over 500 high-energy Sheetz stores throughout six states:
Pennsylvania, Virginia, West Virginia, Maryland, Ohio and North Carolina. And if
you want more options, we have a "universal" card that's accepted at 90% of
fueling locations in the US - anywhere WEX is accepted.

Special Instruction:
Please keep in mind, before applying for multiple accounts with WEX Fleet cards,
please make sure to, have enough time in between applying so that they don't
red flagged your account for fraud.

To Qualify:
-Entity in good standing with Secretary of State
-EIN number with IRS
-Business address- matching everywhere.
-D&B number
-Business License- if applicable
-Business Bank account
-Business Phone Number Listed in 411
-SSN is required for informational purposes. If concerned they will pull your
personal credit please talk. to their credit department before applying.
-Established business credit history
-At least 1 year in business
-If less than 1 year in business will need a Personal Guarantee (PG). Can give a
500 deposit instead of using a PG.

To Apply: Online or over the phone

Terms: Net 15 or Revolving

STAPLES

Staples

Phone: 800-767-1275 (8 am-8 pm ET)

Website: https://www.staples.com/

Reports to: D&B, Experian and Equifax

Description:
Staples is an office products mega-retailer that sells: Office Supplies and Services, Business Machines, Computers and Related Products, and Office Furniture. Online shopping and ordering available or visit a store location.

To Qualify:

Net 30 (Commercial) or Revolving {Business),
-Entity in good standing with Secretary of State
-EIN number with IRS
-Business address- matching everywhere.
-D&B number
-Business License- if applicable
-Business Bank account
-Business Phone Number Listed in 411
-Must have at least 10 employees - Net 30 (Commercial)
-A corporation with more than $5 million annual sales and in business for at least 3years
-If the above criteria are not met, providing a guarantee may increase the likelihood of approval and is recommended if you have a young or small business

To Apply: Online or at the store

Terms: Net 30 and Revolving

Tiger Direct

Phone: 888-278-4437

Website: http://www.tigerdirect.com/

Reports to: D&B, Experian and Equifax

Description:
Tiger Direct is an online provider for everything electronic, office and digital: Computers, Components, Communications, Camcorders, Hard Drives, Laptops, Keyboards, Plasma TV's, Power Supply, Printers, Scanners, Projectors, and much more

To Qualify:
-Entity in good standing with Secretary of State
-EIN number with IRS
-Business address- matching everywhere.
-D&B number
-Business License- if applicable
-Business Bank account
-Bank/trade references
-Business Phone Number Listed in 411
-Should have a business website and a business e-mail.
-At least 2 years in business

To Apply: Online or over the phone 800-364-9485

Terms: Net 30

U-Haul

Phone: 866-333-9731

Website: https://www.uhaul.coml

Reports to: D&B Description:
U-Haul is an American moving equipment and storage rental company, based in Phoenix, Arizona, that has been in operation since 1945. Since 1945, U-Haul has been serving do-it yourself movers and their households.

To Qualify:
-Entity in 900d standing with Secretary of State
-Business credit history
-EIN number with IRS
-Business address- matching everywhere.
-D&B Number
-Business License- if applicable
-Business Bank account
-At least 4 years in business
-Must have a good D&B paydex score of 80 or higher

To Apply: Online

Terms: Net 30

United Rentals

Phone: 888-481-2660

Website: https://www.unitedrentals.com

Reports to: Equifax.

Description:
United Rentals, Inc. is the largest equipment rental company in the world, with an integrated network of more than 900 rental locations in 48 states and 10 Canadian provinces. Their diverse customer base includes construction and industrial companies, utilities, municipalities, government agencies and independent contractors.

To Qualify:
-Entity in good standing with Secretary of State
-EIN number with IRS
-Business address- matching everywhere.
-D&B number
-Business License- if applicable
-Business Bank account
-No minimum time in business
-No minimum purchase to report
-Established business credit history and has the option to apply without a Personal Guarantee (PG}.
-Must have a good Equifax business credit score
-Prefers good Equifax business credit score
-If Equifax business score is low, a PG is required

To Apply: Online or at the local store

Terms: Net 45

Valero

Phone: 844-386-0401

Website: https://www.valero.com/en-us

Reports to: D&B, Experian, and Equifax

Description:
Valero Energy Corporation, through its subsidiaries, is an international manufacturer and marketer of transportation fuels and other petrochemical products.

Special Instruction:
Please keep in mind, before applying for multiple accounts with WEX Fleet cards, please make sure to have enough time in between applying so that they don't red-flagged your account for fraud.

To Qualify:
-Entity in good standing with Secretary of State
-EIN number with IRS
-Business address- matching everywhere.
-D&B number
-Business License- if applicable
-Business Bank account
-Business Phone Number Listed in 411
-They will check the potential client's D & Band Equifax reports.
-SSN is required for informational purposes. If concerned they will pull your personal credit please talk to their credit department before applying.
-If not approved based on business credit history or been in business for less than 1 year, then a $500 deposit 1s needed or a Personal Guarantee (PG)

To Apply; Online

Terms:
Net 26, Revolving (Valero Fleet Card)
Net 15 (Valero Fleet Plus Card)

Tier II Vendors

Valvoline Fleet

Phone: 800-637-1462

Website: https://www.valvoline.com

Reports to: D&B, Experian and Equifax

Description:
Quick, easy, and trusted fleet maintenance by Valvoline instant oil change. Use for maintenance only at Valvoline Instant Oil Change locations. Use for fuel at 90% of fueling locations nationwide-anywhere the WEX card is accepted

Special Instruction:
Please keep in mind, before applying' for multiple accounts with WEX Fleet cards, please make sure to have enough time in between applying so that they don't red-flagged your account for fraud.

To Qualify:

-Entity in good standing with Secretary of State
-EINI number with IRS
-Business address- matching everywhere.
-D&B number
-Business License- if applicable
-Business Bank account
-Business Phone Number Listed in 411
-SSN is required for informational purposes. If concerned they will pull your personal credit please talk to their credit department before applying.
-Trade References
-If not approved based on business credit history or been in business for less than 1 year, then a $500 deposit is needed or a Personal Guarantee (PG)

To Apply: Online or over the phone

Terms: Net 15

Wawa

Phone: 866-553-6065

Website: https://www.wawa.com/
Reports to: D&B, Experian and Equifax Description:
Take control of fleet fueling and other business vehicle-related expenses with the
Wawa Fleet Card. Whether your company has a small fleet or a large fleet, the
Wawa Fleet Card Program is the perfect way to keep your drivers on the road
and on the job.

Special Instruction:
Please keep in mind, before applying for multiple accounts with WEX Fleet cards,
please make sure to, have enough time in between applying so that they don't
red-flag1ged your account for fraud.

To Qualify:
-Entity in good standing with Secretary of State
-EIN number with IRS
-Business address- matching everywhere.
-D&B number
-Business License- if applicable
-Business Bank account
-Business Phone Number Listed in 411
-SSN is required for informational purposes. If concerned they will pull your
personal credit please talk. to their credit department before applying.
-If not approved based on business credit history or been in business less than 1
year then a $500 deposit is needed or a Personal Guarantee (PG)

To Apply: Online

Terms:

Net 1:5 (Wawa Fleet Card, Wawa Universal Card)

Net 26, Revolving {Wawa Flex Fleet Card, Wawa Flex Universal Card)

Zoro

Phone: 855-289-9676

Website: https://www.zoro.com/

Reports to: D&B Description:
Zoro.com is an eCommerce company that sells business supplies, equipment, and tools. We offer Net 30 terms to qualified businesses. These lines of credit allow you time to pay off orders and easily track monthly expenses.

To Qualify:

-Entity in 900d standing with Secretary of State
-EIN number with IRS
-Business address- matching everywhere.
-D&B number
-Business License- if applicable
-Business Bank account
-A business email address where your invoices will be sent
-Strong business credit history with good D&B paydex score of 80 or higher.
-No minimum time in business

To Apply: Over the phone

Terms Net 30

Tier III Vendors

You currently should have 6 trade accounts reporting to your business credit reports.

Now, add 4 more accounts from Tier III.

When you make a purchase, do so on your net/credit terms. It is payments on net/credit terms that are reported.

To ensure that your vendors report your payments, make a purchase of $50 or more.

It typically takes 30-90 days for your payments to report on your business credit reports.

ARCO

Phone: 800-633-3271

Website: https://www.fleetcardsu sa.com

Reports: D&B, Experian and Equifax

Description:
The ARCO Business Solutions program provides more features, benefits and controls for every driver in your fleet. Their Business Solutions Fuel Card provides fleet managers with detailed reporting and individual spending controls. Accepted at over 1,500 participating ARCO locations in the United States ARCO Business Solutions Mastercard gives your drivers the flexibility of fueling at ARCO locations and any other fuel location in the United States where Mastercards are accepted.
Experience complete online control 24/7.

Special Instructions:

The -first payment made to Arco when you have a Net account can take up to 90 days to report. After that it reports monthly.

To Qualify:

Arco Business Solutions Fuel Card or Arco Business Solutions Mastercard
-Entity in good standing with Secretary of State
-EIN number with IRS
-Business address- matching everywhere.
-D&B number
-Business License- if appliable
-Business Bank account
-Business Phone Number Listed in 411
-In Business for at least 1 year
-If not enough business credit history, may ask for a Personal Guarantee (PG)

To Apply: Online or over the phone

Terms: Net 7, Net 10 or Net 15

Tier III Vendors

BP

Phone: 800-348-7959

Website: https://www.bp.com

Reports to: D&B, Experian and Equifax

Description:
BP Business Solutions Fuel Card. Fuel at thousands of BP branded locations in the U.S. Control spending by setting gallon limits for each card. Take charge of your company's fuel expenses by stopping unauthorized purchases and fraud

To Qualify:
-Entity in good standing with Secretary of State
-EIN number with IRS
-Business address- matching everywhere.
-D&B number
-Business License- if applicable
-Business Bank account
Note- If not approved based on merit of application, may ask for deposit or a Personal Guarantee (PG).
-Accepted at thousands of BP or Amoco branded locations in the U.S.

To Apply: Over the phone

Terms Net 7, Net 10 or Net 15

Tier III Vendors

Business T-Shirt Club

Phone: 708-719-4238

Website: https://businesstshirtclub.com/

Reports to: Eqt1ifax

Description:
Business T-Shirt Club is a wholesale t-shirt and apparel buying club exclusively for business owners & entrep1reneurs. Membership grants you access to premium apparel brands at wholesale rates for all your apparel! needs!

To Qualify:
-Entity in good standing with Secretary of State
-EIN number with IRS
-Business address- matching everywhere.
-D&B number
-Business License- if applicable
-Business Bank account
-Minimum order quantity for custom printed apparel is 12 items per design. For blank apparel orders, there is a minimum order amount of $250 required.
-Annual Membership- $69.99

To Apply: Online

Terms - Net 30

CITGO

Phone: 877-596-4342

Website: https://www.citga.com/

Reports to: D&B, Experian and Equifax

Description:
CITGO Petroleum Corporation is a U.S.-based petroleum company with a rich heritage of more than 100 years.
Our history as an American success story began in 1910 with the founding of the Cities Service Company, a then pioneering utility services provider to the sprawling cities of the Midwest. In 1965, our now familiar and enduring CITGO "trimark" brand was born.

Special Instruction:

Please keep in mind, before applying for multiple accounts with WEX Fleet cards, please make sure to have enough time in between applying so that they don't red-flagged your account for fraud.

To Qualify:
-Entity in good standing with Secretary of State
-EIN number with IRS
-Business address- matching everywhere.
-D&B Number
-Business License- if applicable
-Business Bank account
-Business Phone Number Listed in 411
-SSN is required for informational purposes. If concerned they will pull your personal credit please talk to their credit department before applying.
-If not approved based on business credit history or been in business less than 1 year, then a $500 deposit is needed or a Personal Guarantee (PG)

To Apply: Online or over the phone
Terms: Net 15

Crown Office Supplies

Phone: 307-317-7018

Website: http://crownofficesupplies.com/

Reports to: D&B, Experian and Equifax

Description:
Offers a variety of Office Supplies and takes helping clients seriously. They state just starting your business, or maybe have an existing business, but you have a question regarding office supplies... we are here to help!

Special Instruction:

There is a 99.00 annual fee, though they do report that fee to the business credit bureaus. For other purchases to report needs to be a minimum of 30.00 purchase.

To Qualify:
-Entity in good standing with Secretary of State
-EIN number with IRS
-Business address- matching everywhere.
-D&B number
-Business License- if applicable
-Business Bank account
-Business must be at least 90 days old.
-Has other approved vendors with a credit limit of $800 or higher.
-Membership fee is $99 annually upon approval.

To Apply: Online

Terms: Net 30

Gempler's

Phone: 800-382-8473

Website: https://gemplers.com

Reports to: D&B

Description:
Since 1939, Gempler's has been helping outdoor professionals take tough jobs to task. We provide a wide selection of professional-grade tools, equipment, products and supplies., along with easy shopping, dedicated expertise and responsive service. Shop Gempler's for your landscaping, agricultural and pest control needs. Choose from our wide selection of sprayers and accessories for every job. Whether you're a landscape contractor, golf course superintendent, nursery operator or anyone in between, Gempler's can help make your hard work easy.

To Qualify:
-Entity in good standing with Secretary of State
-EIN number with IRS
-Business address- matching everywhere.
-D&N number
-Business License- if applicable
-Business Bank account
-Strong business credit history
-Must have a good D&B paydex score of 80 or higher
-Annual sales with Gempler's of $2500 and 4 or more orders within a 12-month period paid via credit card.

To Apply: over the phone

Terms: Net 30

Lands' End

Phone: 888-462-4705

Website: https://business.landsend.com/

Reports to: D&B

Description:
Trust Lands' End Business Outfitters for all of your business clothing, uniform clothing, corporate gift and promotional product needs. Our top-quality custom logo clothing, corporate apparel and promotional products include embroidered polo shirts, embroidered dress shirts, business outerwear, screen-printed t-shirts and sweatshirts, drinkware, bags, totes and more.

To Qualify:
-Entity in good standing with Secretary of State
-Business credit history
-EIN number with IRS
-Business address- matching everywhere.
-Business License- if applicable
-Business Bank account
-No minimum time in business but needs some credit history established.
-Must have a good D&B Paydex score of 80 or higher

To Apply: Online or over the phone

Terms: Net 30

MAPCO

Website: https://www.fleet-aidvantage.com/

Reports to: D&B, Experian, and Equifax

Description:
MAPCO Fleet is a wholly-owned subsidiary of MAPCO, offering diverse solutions for every type of fleet. They provide industry-leading solutions to companies and fleet managers while creating relationships directly with drivers through their Fleet Rewards program.

Special Instruction:

Please keep in mind, before applying for multiple accounts with WEX Fleet cards, please make sure to have enough time in between applying so that they don't red-flagged your account for fraud.

To Qualify:
-Entity in good standing with Secretary of State
-EIN number with IRS
-Business address- matching everywhere.
-D&B number
-Business License- if applicable
-Business Bank account
-Business Phone Number Listed in 411
-SSN is required for informational purposes. If concerned they will pull your personal credit please talk to their credit department before applying.
-If not approved based on business credit history or been in business less than 1 year, then a $500 deposit is needed or a Personal Guarantee (PG)

To Apply: Online or over the phone

Terms: Net 15

Tier III Vendors

NTB

Phone: 888-313-5338

Website: https://www.ntb.com/home

Reports to: D&B

Description:
We strive to be a go-to resource for your cars health. With a huge range of tires and quality products at the guaranteed lowest price, combined with fast, hassle-free service, our bumper-to-bumper auto care is all you need, every time. Whenever your vehicle requires service or repair, you can trust our highly qualified technicians to get you back on the road. We'll even help you remember the important to-dos like, oil changes and routine service. Plus, we can send you coupons to help keep your costs down, just in time.

To Qualify:
-Entity in good standing with Secretary of State
-Business credit history
-EIN number with IRS
-Business address- matching everywhere.
-Business License- if applicable
-Business Bank account
-Bank references
-Trade references
-Must have a 9100d D&B paydex score of 80 or higher

To Apply· Online or over the phone

Terms: Net 30

ORR Safety

Phone: 800-669-1677

Website: https://www.on-safety.com/

Reports to: D&B

Description:
ORR Safety Corporation is a family-owned distributor of Personal Protective Equipment (IPPE} and related services to the industrial market. Since 1948 ORR Safety has provided products and services to over 20,000 companies, helping to protect hundreds of thousands of workers. ORR Safety continues to partner with companies to achieve the passion possessed by all of us-to provide a safe work environment and protect workers from the possibility-of injury.

To Qualify:
-Entity in good standing with Secretary of State
-EIN number with IRS
-Business address- matching everywhere.
-D&B number
-Business License- if applicable
-Business Bank account
-Business Phone Number Listed in 411
-Trade/credit references
-Must have a good D&B paydex score of 80 o-r higher
-At least 2 years in business

To Apply·
Over the phone - 502.774.6557 {credit dept.)
and Fax, mail or e-mail the credit application.

Fax: 502.515.8-020
Mailing Address: PO Box 198029, Louisville, KY 40259-8029
E-mail: CreditDepartment@orrcorp.com

Terms: Net 30

platt.com

Platt

Phone: 503-526-2326

Website: https://www.platt.com

Reports to: D&B and Experian

Description:
Platt Electric Supply is a. wholesale distributor of electrical, industrial, lighting, tools, control and automation products for the electrical, construction, commercial, industrial, utility and datacom markets.

To Qualify:
-Entity in good standing with Secretary of State
-EIN number with IRS
-Business address- matching everywhere.
-D&B number
-Business License- if applicable
-Business Bank account
-No minimum accounts reporting1- overall review
-Must have a good D&B paydex score of 80 or higher
-No minimum time in Business

To Apply: Online

Terms - Net 30

Royal Farms

Phone: 888-300-9034

Website: https://www.royalfarms.com

Reports to: D&B, Experian and Equifax

Description:
Since 1959, this is your go-to place day or night for breakfast, lunch, snacks, dinner, gasoline and diesel fuel, and all the things you need Dine in our seating area or take out.

Special Instruction:
Please keep in mind, before applying' for multiple accounts with WEX Fleet cards, please make sure to have enough time in between applying so that they don't red-flagged your account for fraud. Please apply within .2 to 3 months apart per application.

To Qualify:

-Entity in good standing with Secretary of State
-EIN number with IRS
-Business address- matching everywhere.
-D&B number
-Business License- if applicable
-Business Bank account
-Business Phone Number Listed in 411
-SSN is required for informational purposes. If concerned they will pull your personal credit please talk to their credit department before applying.
-If not approved based on business credit history or been in business less than 1 year, then a $500 deposit is needed or a Personal Guarantee (PG)

To Apply: Online or over the phone

Terms: Net 15

Tier III Vendors

Shell

Phone: 888-260-0886

Website: https://www.shell.us

Reports to: D&B, Experian and Equifax

Description:
Shell is a global group of energy and petrochemical companies. A Shell
Card will help you keep vehicles in shape and your expenses under control.

Special Instruction:

Please keep in mind, before applying' for multiple accounts with WEX Fleet
cards, please make sure to have enough time in between applying so
that they don't red-flagged your account for fraud.

To Qualify:
-Entity in good standing with Secretary of State
-EIN number with IRS
-Business address- matching everywhere.
-D&B number
-Business License- if applicable
-Business Bank account
-Business Phone Number Listed in 411
-SSN is required for informational purposes. If concerned they will pull
your
personal credit please talk to their credit department before applying.
-If not approved based on business credit history or been in business less
than 1 year, then a $500 deposit 1s needed or a Personal Guarantee (PG)

To Apply: Online or over the phone

Terms: Net 15

Tier III Vendors

Sinclair

Phone: 866-300-5469

Website: https://www.sinclairoil.com

Reports to: D&B, Experian and Equifax

Description:
Sinclair Oil Corporation has been helping western America drive with confidence for over 80 years.!

Special Instruction:
Please keep in mind, before applying for multiple accounts with WEX Fleet cards, please make sure to have enough time in between applying so that they don't red-flagged your account for fraud.

To Qualify:
-Entity in good standing with Secretary of State
-EIN number with IRS
-Business address- matching everywhere.
-D&N number
-Business License- if applicable
-Business Bank account
-Business Phone Number Listed in 411
-SSN is required for informational purposes. If concerned they will pull your personal credit please talk to their credit department before applying.
-If not approved based on business credit history or been in business less than 1 year, then a $500 deposit is needed or a Personal Guarantee (PG)

To Apply: Online

Terms: Net 15

Tier III Vendors

Speedway

Phone: 866-885-4965

Website: https://www.speedway.com

Reports to: D&B and Experian

Description:
Speedway is a gasoline-convenience store company with over 4,000 stores from coast to coast. At Speedway, we are proud of our success at meeting the fueling and convenience needs of over two million customers every day, and proud of the reputation of our good name within the communities we serve. Speedway is a wholly owned subsidiary of Marathon Petroleum Corporation.

To Qualify:

-Entity in good standing with Secretary of State
-EIN number with IRS
-Business address- matching everywhere.
-D&B number
-Business License- if applicable
-Business Bank account
-At least 1 year in business
-Good business payment history, approves on overall merit of application
-Can use a Personal Guarantee (PG) or $500 deposit if not approved with EIN

To Apply: Online or over the phone

Terms: Net 15

Tier III Vendors

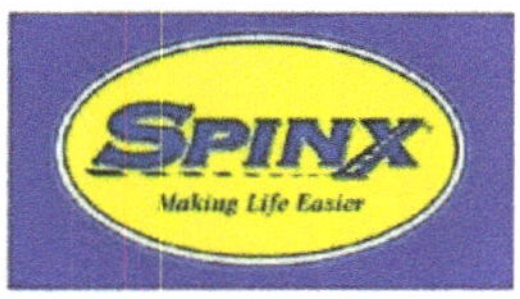

Spinx

Phone: 800-950-5074

Website: https://www.myspinx.com

Reports to: D&B, Experian and Equifax

Description:
The Spinx Fleet Services Card, powered by WEX. To prevent unauthorized fueling, each vehicle is assigned a card and each driver is assigned a unique identification number-one cannot be used without the other. You decide who can purchase what, when, and how much. Simple, easy-to-read monthly reports, available online and in paper formats, show how and where your vehicles were fueled, so you can account for every penny. No annual fee but with a monthly fee of $2 per card.

Special Instruction:
Please keep in mind, before applying 'for multiple accounts with WEX Fleet cards, please make sure to have enough time in between applying so that they don't red-flagged your account for fraud. Please apply within 2 to 3 months apart per application.

To Qualify:
-Entity in good standing with Secretary of State
-EIN number with IRS
-Business address- matching everywhere.
-D&N business
-Business License- if applicable
-Business Bank account
-Business Phone Number Listed in 411
-SSN is required for informational purposes. If concerned they will pull your personal credit please talk to their credit department before applying.
-If not approved based on business credit history or been in business less than 1 year, then a $500 deposit is needed or a Personal Guarantee(PG)

To Apply: Online

Terms: Net 15

Stripes Fleet

Phone: 866-325-6961

Website: https://www.stripesfleetcards.com/

Reports to: D&B, Experian and Equifax

Description:
The Stripes fleet card program is designed to help businesses optimize savings, receive competitive fuel rebates at Stripes Stores, and fuel almost anywhere in the U.S.

Special Instruction:

Please keep in mind, before applying for multiple accounts with WEX Fleet cards, please make sure to, have enough time in between applying so that they don't red flagged your account for fraud.

To Qualify:
-Entity in good standing with Secretary of State
-EIN number with IRS
-Business address- matching everywhere.
-D&B number
-Business License- if applicable
-Business Bank account
-Business Phone Number Listed in 411
-SSN is required for informational purposes. If concerned they will pull your personal credit please talk. to their credit department before applying.
-If not approved based on business credit history-or been in business less than 1 year then a $500 deposit is needed or a Personal Guarantee (PG)

To Apply: Online or over the phone

Terms: Net 15

Summa Office Supplies

Phone: 818-476--7892
Website: https://s mmaofficesupplies.com/ apply

Reports to:
Tier 1 account reports to Equifax
Tier 2 account reports to D&B

Description:
Summa Office Supplies is the ultimate source for all of your office product needs. We specialize in quality office products and supplies at guaranteed savings. We are ready to provide you and your team with the quality office supply products that are essential to your office environment.

Special Note:
Tier 1 account only has limited options of products. but is able to get with not many
qualifications.

Tier 2 account offers their full list of products but might ask for a PG

To Qualify:
-Offer Net 30 with normal Biz foundation- $2000 limit
-Min $75.00 purchase for the first order only to report
-Entity in good standing with Secretary of State
-EIN number with IRS
-Business address- matching everywhere.
-D&B number
-Business License- if applicable
-Business Bank account
-You may qualify for Tier 1 account if new in business and not enough business credit history with a minimum order of $80 of downloadable products.
-You may qualify for Tier 2 account if the business has 6 months or more of credit reporting with a minimum order of $300 worth of office supplies upon checkout.

To Apply: Online

Terms: Net 30

Tier III Vendors

Sunoco

Phone:844-255-4520

Website: https://www.sunoco.com

Reports to: D&B, Experian and Equifax

Description:
Sunoco Corporate Gas Card. This no-fee card helps smaller fleets control fuel
cost by eliminating unwanted purchases and supplying transaction-level
purchase.

To Qualify:
Sunoco Suntrak Card and Sunoco Universal Card
-Entity in good standing with Secretary of State
-EIN number with IRS
-Business address- matching everywhere.
-D&B number
-Business License- if applicable
-Business Bank account
-Business Phone Number Listed in 411
-SSN is, required for informational purposes. If concerned they will pull your
personal credit please talk to their credit department before applying.
-If not approved based on business credit history or been in business less than 1
year, then a $500 deposit is needed or a Personal Guarantee (PG)

Sunoco Corporate Card
-Same as above except:
-At least 3 years in the business
-Has an annual revenue of $1M or more

To Apply: Online or over the phone

Terms:
Net 15 (Sunoco Suntrak Card and Universal Fleet Card),

Revolving (Sunoco Corporate Card)

Tractor Supply

Phone: 800-559-8232

Website: https://www.tractorsupply.com

Reports to: D&B and Experian

Description:
Tractor Supply is the largest rural lifestyle retailer in the United States, has been passionate about serving its unique niche, as a one-stop shop for recreational farmers, ranchers and all those who enjoy living the rural lifestyle, for more than 80 years.

To Qualify:

Net 30, 60 terms
-Entity in good standing with Secretary of State
-EIN number with IRS
-Business address- matching everywhere.
-D&B number
-Business License- if applicable
-Business Bank account
-Should been in business for at least 6 months
-Must have a good D&B paydex score of 80 or higher
-A Personal Guarantee (PG) is NOT required

Revolving
-Entity in good standing with Secretary of State
-EIN number with IRS
-Business address- matching everywhere.
-D&B number
-Business License- if applicable
-Business Bank account
-No minimum time in business
-A Personal Guarantee (PG) is required

To Apply: Online or at the store

Terms: Net 30, Net 60 or Revolving

Tier IV Vendors

You currently should have 10 trade accounts reporting to your business credit reports.

Now, add 4 more accounts from Tier IV.

When you make a purchase, do so on your net/credit terms. It is payments on net/credit terms that are reported.

To ensure that your vendors report your payments, make a purchase of $50 or more.

It typically takes 30-90 days for your payments to report on your business credit reports.

ABC Supply Co.

Phone: 608-802-3068

Website: https://www.abcsupply.com

Reports to: Experian and Equifax

Description:
ABC Supply Co., Inc. is the largest wholesale distributor of roofing in the United States and one of the nation's largest distributors of siding, windows and other select exterior and interior building products, tools and related supplies. Since our start in 1982., we've grown to become a national organization with more than 700 branches and other facilities in 49 states.

Our success is the result of an unwavering focus on a single, simple guiding principle - treat contractors {large and small) with respect and give them the products and services they need to build their businesses. We offer high quality products, superior service and competitive pricing, ensuring the contractors have the products they need - when and where they need them.

To Qualify:
-Entity in good standing with Secretary of State
-EIN number with IRS
-Business address- matching everywhere.
-D&B number
-Business License- if applicable
-Business Bank account
-Trade account reference required.
-Some established business credit history
-If not enough business credit history, a Personal Guarantee (PG} is required

To Apply: Online-
Print and complete the application and return it or fax it to your local ABC Supply branch.
or send via email: cfs961@abcsupply.com

Terms: Net 30

Ally

Phone: 888-925-2559

Website: https://www.ally.com

Reports to: D&B, Experian and Equifax

Description:
Ally offers commercial vehicle financing. Gives personal financing but reports also to business credit bureaus If your business qualifies for financing without the owner's guaranty, you can obtain financing in the business name only. This gives you the ability to save your personal credit for other use as well.

To Qualify:

-Entity in good standing with Secretary of State
-EIN number with IRS
-Business address- matching everywhere.
-D&B number
-Business License- if applicable
-Business Bank account
-Bank reference
-Fleet financing references
-Apply in business only, dealer will advise if approved or Personal Guarantee (PG) needed
-If PG is used will not report on personal bureaus, unless account defaults

To Apply: At Dealership only. dealer locations listed on their website.

Terms: Lease or Loan

Tier IV Vendors

American Express

Phone: 8SS-854-2688

Website:https://www.americanexpress.com/us/credit-cards/business/corporate-credit-cards/?inav=footer_corp_pirg

Reports to: D&B

Description:
American Express offers world-class Charge and Credit Cards, Gift Cards,
Rewards, Travel, Personal Savings, Business Services, Insurance and more

To Qualify:
AMEX Corporate Start-up Account
-Entity in good standing with Secretary of State
-EIN number with IRS
-Business address- matching everywhere.
-D&B number
-Business License- if applicable
-Business Bank account
-Bank statement for the last 3 months, with a minimum of $2 million bank account
balance.

AMEX Corporate Account
-Entity in good standing with Secretary of State
-EIN number with IRS
-Business address- matching everywhere.
-D&B number
-Business License- if applicable
-Business Bank account
-Has a minimum of $4M in annual revenue
-At least 2 years of financial statement

To Apply: Online or over the phone

Terms: Net 30

Brex

Phone: 844-725-9569

Website: https://brex.com/

Reports to: D&B and Experian

Description:
Brex is rebuilding IB2B financial products, starting with a corporate card for technology companies. We help startups of all sizes (from recently incorporated to later-stage companies) to instantly get a card that has 20x higher limits, completely automates expense management, kills receipt tracking, and magically integrates with their accounting systems.

Special Instruction::

They offer 2 types of business credit account- for Start-up businesses and E-commerce. They don't offer balance transfer from other credit cards to Brex due to Non-PG.

To Qualify:
-Entity in good standing with Secretary of State
-EIN number with IRS
-Business address- matching everywhere.
-D&B number
-Business License- if applicable
-Business Bank account
-No Personal Guarantee is required.

-For Start-Up Account:
-No minimum time in business
-Average bank balance of $1100,000 ·to get approved for Net 3,0
-Average bank balance of $50,000 and below with Professional Investors like Venture Capital and Private Equity.

To Apply: Online

Terms -Net 30

Tier IV Vendors

Cenex

Phone: 800-852-5301

Website: https://www.cenex.com

Reports to: Equifax

Description:
CENEX have a fleet and business card. Both are private labeled and can only be
used at the store/ station.

To Qualify:
Cenex Business credit card or Cenex Voyager Fleet card
-Entity in good standing with Secretary of State
-EIN number with IRS
-Business address- matching everywhere.
-D&B number
-Business License- if applicable
-Business Bank account
-Bank references
-Been in business for at least 3 years
-If less than 3 years, a Personal Guarantee (PG) is required
-No Florida and CA PG allowed

To Apply: Online or over the phone (800-852-8180)

Terms: Net 25

Tier IV Vendors

Circle K

Phone: 866-462-5035

Website: https://www.circlek.com

Reports to: D&B, Experian and Equifax

Description:
Circle K offers a private labeled fleet card with the Circle K Fleet Card, you can
save up to 4c a gallon (based on monthly gallons purchased at Circle K
locations).

Special Instruction:

Please keep in mind, before applying for multiple accounts with WEX Fleet cards,
please make sure to have enough time in between applying so that they don't
red-flagged your account for fraud.

To Qualify:

-Entity in good standing with Secretary of State
-EIN number with IRS
-Business address- matching everywhere.
-D&B number
-Business License- if applicable
-Business Bank account
-Business Phone Number Listed in 411
-SSN is required for informational purposes. If concerned they will pull your
personal credit please talk to their credit department before applying.
-If not approved based on business credit history or been in business less than 1
year then a $500 deposit is needed or a Personal Guarantee (PG)

To Apply: Online or over the phone (800) 852-8180

Terms: Net 15

Tier IV Vendors

Chevron/Texaco

Phone: 888-531-3717

Website: https://www.chevron.com

Reports to: D&B, Experian and Equifax

Description:
Chevron /Texaco Universal Business Card gives you a turn-key system1to help control and monitor fuel expenses. The Business Card is accepted at thousands of Chevron and Texaco stations for gasoline, tires, batteries, and more.

Special Instruction:

Please keep in mind, before applying for multiple accounts with WEX Fleet cards, please make sure to have enough time in between applying so that they don't red-flagged your account for fraud.

To Qualify:
-Entity in good standing with Secretary of State
-EIN number with IRS
-Business address- matching everywhere.
-D&B number
-Business License- if applicable
-Business Bank account
-Business Phone Number Listed in 411
-Established business credit
-Prefer in business for over 18 months.
If not approved based on business credit history or been in business for less than 1
-1/2 years, then a $500 deposit is needed or a Personal Guarantee (PG)

To Apply: Online or over the phone

Terms: Net 7

Citizens Bank

Phone: 866-248-4936 ext. 2

Website: https://www.citizensbank.com/small-business/overview.aspx

Reports to: D&B, Experian and Equifax

Description:
As the 13th largest retail bank in the United States, we deliver a broad range of financial services to over five million individuals, companies, not for profits, and institutions.

To Qualify:
-Entity in good standing with Secretary of State
-EIN number with IRS
-Business address- matching everywhere.
-D&B number
-Business License- if applicable
-Business Bank account
-Social security number
-Trade reference
-A Personal Guarantee (PG) is required.
-Minimum of 6 months in business
-Business must be located in RII, MA, CT, DE, MI, PA, NJ., NY, OH, PA, RI, VT AND NH

To Apply: Online, over the phone or at the branch

Terms: Revolving

Commerce Bank

Phone: 800-892-7104 option 2

Website: https://www.commercebank.com/

Reports to: D&B and Experian

Description:
At Commerce Bank, we have over 150 years of experience and many strong, established products to back us up. From Bloomington, Illinois to Denver, Colorado, and at 184 branches in between, we serve individuals, families, businesses and communities at the local branch, the ATM, online and through our 24/7 customer service line. Commerce Bank serves customers in Missouri, Kansas, Illinois, Oklahoma, and Colorado.

To Qualify:
-Entity in good standing with Secretary of State
-Business credit history·
-EIN number with IRS
-Business address- matching everywhere.
-D&B number
-Business License- if applicable
-Business Bank account
-No minimum time in business
-Must have at least $SM in annual revenue
-If less than $SM in annual revenue, a Personal Guarantee (PG) is required.
-For profit businesses with annual revenue of SS million or greater may choose to be underwritten based on company liability, provided that financial statements and a Corporate Resolution are also submitted.
-Any business within Commerce Bank's retail lending area (MO, KS, IL, OK, CO) only can apply.
-Cash advance available with business credit card approval, amount of cash advance depends upon approval amount.

To Apply: At a branch if online they may require a PG

Terms: Net 30 or Revolving

Tier IV Vendors

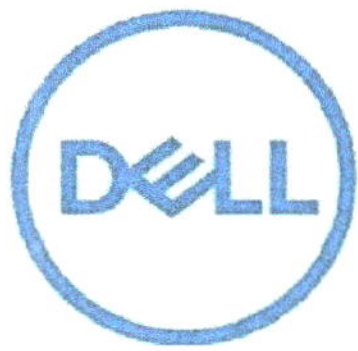

Dell

Phone:512-513-3276

Website: https://www.dell.com/en-us

Reports to: D&B – Quarterly

Description:
Visit Dell to buy computers and accessories for your Home or Small, Medium &
Large Business. The Dell Business Credit Account is a revolving line of credit
that provides an easy way to finance purchases of Dell equipment.

To Qualify:

-Entity in good standing with Secretary of State
-EINI number with IRS
-Business address- matching everywhere.
-D&B number
-Business License- if applicable
-Business Bank account
-Good Business Credit, no minimum
-3-5 years in Business
-Personal Guarantee (IPG) may be required if some criteria is not met

To Apply: Online or over the phone

Terms Revolving

Divvy

Phone: 385-352-0374

Website: https://getdivvy.com/

Reports to: D&B

Description:
Divvy is the leading spend and expense management platform for business. It's fused with a smart corporate credit card to provide instant visibility and control of companywide spending. With Divvy, employers can give employees direct access to funds, effectively eliminating expense reports and retroactive reimbursements.

To Qualify:
-Entity in good standing with Secretary of State
-Business credit history
-EIN number with IRS
-Business address- matching everywhere.
-D&B Number
-Business License- if applicable
-Business Bank account
-Business Bank Statement
-No minimum time in business
-Trade/credit references
-Must have a good D&B paydex score of 80 or higher
-Has the option to apply without a Personal Guarantee {PG).

To Apply· Online

Terms: Net 7, Net 15 or Net 30

Tier IV Vendors

Frost Bank

Phone: 866-376-7889

Website: https://www.frostbank.com/

Reports to: D&B and Experian

Description:
Everyone is significant, and at Frost, we treat them that way. We give our customers a square deal and keep their assets safe and sound. These beliefs have guided Frost from the very beginning and served our customers well since 1868. We offer our customers a full range of banking, investment and insurance products to help them better manage their money, grow their wealth and protect their assets. And our disciplined relationship approach has stood the test of time.

To Qualify:
-Entity in good standing with Secretary of State
-Business credit history·
-EIN number with IRS
-Business address- matching everywhere.
-D&B number
-Business License- if applicable
-Business Bank account
-No minimum time in business
-Must have at least $5M in annual revenue
-If less than $5M in annual revenue, a Personal Guarantee (PG) is required.
-For profit businesses with annual revenue of SS million or greater may choose to be underwritten based on company liability, provided that financial statements and a Corporate Resolution are also submitted.
-Businesses that are registered in Texas state only are eligible to apply.
-Must be a current Frost customer only to apply.

To Apply: At a branch if online they may require a PG

Terms: Revolving

Irving

Phone: 866-999-8199

Website: https://www.theirving.com

Reports to: D&B and Equifax

Description:
Protect your account with improved security features such as odometer prompts and driver ID validation. Choose the control option that best meets your needs

Fuel only - Restricts card purchases to fuel only.
Open to buy - Allows both fuel and convenience store purchases.

To Qualify:
-Entity in good standing with Secretary of State
-EIN number with IRS - Business address- matching everywhere
-D&B number
-Business License- if applicable
-Business Bank account
-Bank reference
-Business phone no. listing to 411
-Strong business credit history with good D&B score.
-Been in business for at least 2 years
-Note- If not approved based on merit of application, may ask for deposit or Personal Guarantee (PG).

To Apply· Online

Terms: Net 7, Net 15 or Net 30

Tier IV Vendors

Sam Ash

Phone: 800-472-6274

Website: https://www.samash.com/

Reports to: D&B and Experian

Description:
Sam Ash Music Direct is a nationwide online music store that sells guitars, basses, drums, live sound and recording equipment

To Qualify:
-Entity in good standing with Secretary of State
-EIN number with IRS
-Business address- matching everywhere.
-D&B number
-Business License- if applicable
-Business Bank account
-Trade references
-Bank references
-Gross Annual Sales
-Must have a good D&B paydex score of 80 or higher.
-At least 2 years in business, if less than 2 years in business, a Personal Guarantee (PG) is required.

To Apply; Over the phone (856) 505-4192 or at the store

Terms: Net 30

Tier IV Vendors

Sam's Club

Phone: 800-362-6196

Website: https://www.samsclub.com/sams/homepage.jsp

Reports to: D&B

Description:
Sam's Club is a warehouse retail chain offering office supplies, business furniture, vending items, janitorial/cleaning supplies, paper products, food service supplies, computers, and more.

To Qualify:

-Entity in good standing with Secretary of State
-EIN number with IRS
-Business address- matching everywhere.
-D&B number
-Business License- if applicable
-Business Bank account
-Business Phone Number Listed in 411
-Must have Club membership

As stated on their application if less than the below items might be harder to be approved without a Personal Guarantee (PG) but can try

-$5 million in annual sales or revenues
-At least 2 years in business
-More than 10 employees
-A Personal Guarantee (PG) is required if company is a Sole Proprietor or Partnership
-Cash advance available with business credit card approval, amount of cash advance depends upon approval amount.

To Apply: At the store

Terms: Revolving

Tier IV Vendors

Sutherlands

Phone:816-756-3000

Website: https://sutherlands.com

Reports to: D&B

Description:
The Sutherland lumber Company is a privately-owned, family run organization founded 100 years ago by Robert R. Sutherland. They specialize in complete building packages, including storage sheds, garages, post frame buildings and pole barns, and entire houses. Sutherland's staff of knowledgeable experts can help plan any project, large or small.

To Qualify:

-Entity in good standing with Secretary of State
-EIN number with IRS
-Business address- matching everywhere.
-D&B number
-Business License- if applicable
-Business Bank account
-Number of Employees
-Apply in business only, they will advise if approved or PG needed
-If not approved based on business credit history, a Personal Guarantee (PG) is required.
-Cash advance available with business credit card approval, amount of cash advance depends upon approval amount.

To Apply: Online or at the store

Terms: Revolving

Tier IV Vendors

Tesoro

Phone: 888-367-8417

Website: http://www.tesorofteet.com

Reports to: D&B, Experian and Equifax

Description:
Tesoro commercial fleet fuel and universal cards will save your business time and money. Save at over 70 Tesoro locations in Alaska. Get what you need to rein in one of your biggest business expenses, with automatic, accounting, reports, and powerful tools for saving.

Special Instruction:

Please keep in mind, before applying for multiple accounts with WEX Fleet cards, please make sure to have enough time in between applying so that they don't red-flagged your account for fraud.

To Qualify:
-Entity in good standing with Secretary of State
-EIN number with IRS
-Business address- matching everywhere.
-D&B number
-Business License- if applicable
-Business Bank account
-Business Phone Number Listed in 411
-SSN is required for informational purposes. If concerned they will pull your personal credit, please talk to their credit department before applying.
-If not approved based on business credit history or been in business less than 1 year, then a $500 deposit is needed or a Personal Guarantee (PG)

To Apply: Online or over the phone

Terms: Net 15

Thorntons

Phone: 800-928-8022

Website: https://www.thorntonsinc.com

Reports to: D&B, Experian and Equifax

Description:
Thorntons strives daily to be our guests' favorite place to stop when they are on-the-go. As a family and Team Member-owned, privately held company, our team-based, high-energy culture is a combination of entrepreneurial spirit and core values centered around our guests.

Special Instruction:

Please keep in mind, before applying for multiple accounts with WEX Fleet cards, please make sure to have enough time in between applying so that they don't red-flagged your account for fraud.

To Qualify:
-Entity in good standing with Secretary of State
-EIN number with IRS
-Business address- matching everywhere.
-D&B number
-Business License- if applicable
-Business Bank account
-Business Phone Number Listed in 411
-SSN is required for informational purposes. If concerned they will pull your personal credit please talk to their credit department before applying.
-If not approved based on business credit history or been in business less than 1 year, then a $500 deposit is needed or a Personal Guarantee (PG)

To Apply: Online or over the phone

Terms: Net 15

Toyota

Phone: 800-331-4331

Website: https://www.toyota.com/

Reports to: Experian and Equifax

Descript ion:
Toyota Motor Corporation is a global automotive industry leader manufacturing vehicles in 27 countries or regions and marketing the company's products in over 170 countries and regions. Founded in 1937 and headquartered in Toyota City, Japan, Toyota Motor Corporation employs nearly 350,000 people globally.

To Qualify:
-Entity in good standing with Secretary of State
-EIN number with IRS
-Business address- matching everywhere.
-D&B number
-Business License if applicable
-Business Bank account
-Bank reference
-Trade/credit references
-Good business credit history
-At least 2 years in business
-If not approved based on business credit history or been in business less than 2 years, then a Personal Guarantee (PG) is required.

To Apply: At the dealership - https://www.toyoto.com/dealers/

Terms: Revolving

If you may be interested in our Done for you Business Credit and Funding service visit us at:

Premier1BusinessCredit.com